The Great Healthy Yard Project

The Great Healthy Yard  Project

OUR YARDS, OUR CHILDREN, OUR RESPONSIBILITY

Diane Lewis, M. D.

Published 2014
Printed in the United States of America
ISBN: 978-1-938314-86-5
Library of Congress Control Number: 2014930750

For information, address:
She Writes Press
1563 Solano Ave #546
Berkeley, CA 94707

Interior design by Tabitha Lahr

TO my husband, Blair, and my friend Susanne, who encouraged me to write this book. To Blair, Mack, and Maggie, for your patience while I worked on it. To my friend Lucy, who understood this before all of the rest of us.

Contents

Introduction

I grew up in the Bronx, near the Hudson River. I spent many afternoons at a neighbor's home, perched high on an open, grassy hill overlooking the river, watching thunderstorms roll in over the Palisades. I fell asleep to the sound of tugboats on the river, but I was never allowed near the water itself. The Hudson was laden with viruses, bacteria, and dead fish. Though the river helped establish my love of the natural world, it was also my first experience with a toxic environment.

About the age of twelve, I was playing near the river with some friends and we decided to climb the stone wall and imposing wrought-iron fence that surrounded an abandoned estate. We found two beautiful old mansions filled, not with furniture and paintings, but murky fish tanks, fishing nets, and terrifying specimens from the Hudson River. We had stumbled onto the Wave Hill Center for Environmental Studies. Rather than reprimanding us, Wave Hill enlisted our help and not only awakened in me a deep respect for the natural world but also the conviction that what is seemingly insurmountable can be accomplished.

In their work, Wave Hill made small but tangible improvements in the health of the Hudson River, which I had previously believed was irreparably damaged. I went back to the mansion day after day to lend my hand with minor tasks, driven by a feeling of empowerment—I was making a difference in a positive way. This sentiment was the foundation of my involvement in the environmental movement. At the time, I was still unaware of the extent to which polluted water affects us. I later learned that the Hudson River harbored PCBs—a deadly, invisible, manmade poison that had been discharged into the river during the manufacture of electrical equipment. The effects of this were dormant for years, and people only knew they were sick decades later, when diagnosed with cancer.

I grew up in the era of Silent Spring, Love Canal, and DES. I knew the world was dangerous, but was made to feel that these dangers were containable. I have learned that this is not true. We are inextricably linked with all aspects of the natural world, and because of this, pollution puts us all at risk every day.

When I became a mother, I initially thought feeding my children natural foods and spending time in the wilderness would protect them, but I learned that this, too, wasn't true. Failed exams, broken bones, and bad relationships can be fixed.

Exposure to environmental toxins cannot. As a mother I felt the need to take constructive action to protect my children. With this in mind, and because my husband and I wanted our children to develop a strong connection to the natural world, our children grew up spending their vacations, four months a year, on the shores of a river in the Adirondacks, away from the congestion and pollution of New York City and its suburbs.

Floating downriver in small boats, our children were consumed with laughter and mischief as they overturned their kayaks and rushed dangerously close to sharp rocks and protruding tree stubs. I was constantly torn between appreciating their freedom and wanting to shield them from danger. Rocks and boulders in the river had destroyed one of our more fragile canoes; they would not be good for little heads. So I taught my children how to circumvent danger, and how to drift to the oxbow, where the river slowed, to recapture their kayaks.

Far from New York City, I thought my children were safe; I didn't know then that the river carried dangers more difficult to protect against than rocks. The river appeared to be clean, but it wasn't. It had treated sewage that the nearest town released into a river that drained into ours. Storm water runoff laden with fertilizers and pesticides from a golf course also drained into the river. An old dump near the shore leached chemicals upriver, and nearby potato farmers frequently sprayed their crops on the flood plain. Yet the state stocked the river with trout for people to fish . . . and eat. Even after my children climbed out of the river, they were not safe.

As a nephrologist, I understand not only the importance of clean water but also the impact chemicals have on the body. The Clean Water Act was passed in 1972 to preserve clean water and prevent companies from discharging large amounts of toxic waste into waterways. Unregulated industries don't pose the same kind

ADOPT YOUR WATERSHED!

After our children were grown, when my husband and I rearranged our lives and returned to living full time in Bedford, New York, I was given a leadership role in a newly founded nonprofit called Bedford 2020. (I am currently chair of their Water and Land Use Task Force.) At the time, I was asked to devise ways to protect these two intimately related resources (water and land). To emphasize the inextricable link between water quality and land stewardship, one of my first projects was to organize a tree planting that demonstrated that what we do locally not only impacts our local groundwater wells and streams, but also the water quality of other communities.

I also worked with the town and local land trust to develop a color-coded map of the watersheds, big enough so that individuals could locate their own homes. At the talk where the map was unveiled, residents were given color-coded nametags and were seated together with members of their own watershed.

Neighbors got to know one another and a dialogue around water began. The Great Healthy Yard Project was born when I realized that educating the broader community would have an even bigger impact on protecting water quality.

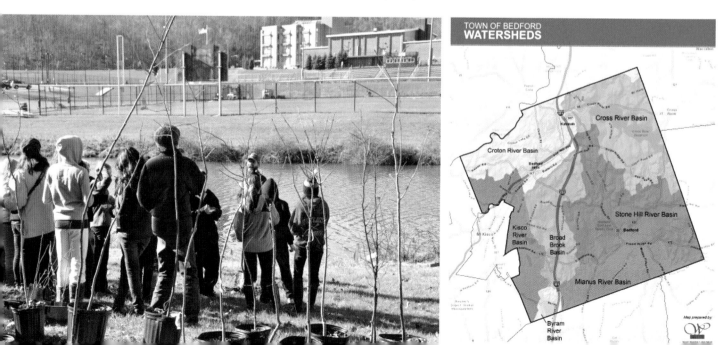

of threat to our health and water they once did. Ironically, we consumers are now one of the primary culprits. Recent research shows that much of the pollution affecting our health and water quality today is due to residential use of chemical pesticides, weed killers, and fertilizers.

The goal of The Great Healthy Yard Project is to educate people about the specific ways in which lawn and garden chemicals end up in the water supply and affect health. It also offers simple alternatives to promote the practice of Minimal Impact Management, or caring for your yard (or property) with the least possible disruption to the natural ecosystem in order to protect waterways, native plants, and wildlife. A cumulative, substantial, and quantifiable improvement can be made to our water supply, and thus health, if we simply refrain from the use of these chemicals and encourage our communities to do the same.

This book is not about absolutes; it's about making small, constructive changes every day. It is my hope that as more people understand the hazards of commonly used chemicals—and their viable alternatives—making these changes will become a mainstream effort.

Take "The Pledge!"

CHAPTER I:

The Myth of the Emerald Green Lawn

"There's a snake lurking in the grass."
—Virgil, Eclogues (3.93)

Big or small, our yards are important to us. They frame our homes and welcome friends and family. Our families grow up in our yards, running through sprinklers and learning how to throw a ball or turn a cartwheel. Our lawns are where we can go barefoot after a long week at work and have neighbors over for barbecues on summer evenings to get to know our community. Gardening in our yards is one of the few ways many of us still get to work with and experience nature. So it's not surprising that many of us want our yards to be beautiful. But most would be surprised to discover that how we care for our yards has a big impact on our water quality.

The chemicals we use on our yards are one of the largest sources of pollution contaminating our drinking water today.

Many of us don't connect our yards with our drinking water or water supply, but the chemicals we use on our lawns and gardens wash with rain and storm water into our streams, lakes, reservoirs, and even our deep groundwater wells, in measurable amounts. Together, these water sources comprise our drinking water—and as a result, chemicals flow into our homes and bodies.

Two landmark studies published in 2013

make it clear that the state of our drinking water supply is a national crisis. The first National Assessment of Rivers and Streams, conducted by the Environmental Protection Agency, concluded that more than half of the rivers and streams nationally, and up to 71 percent in the East and Midwest regions, are of poor quality to support aquatic life due largely to chemical runoff from lawn and garden fertilizers.[1] In addition, a study by the United States Geological Survey found at least one pesticide, and often more than one, in almost every surface water and fish sample tested and in half of the samples drawn from deep groundwater wells throughout the country.[2] These studies demonstrate that the chemicals we use in our yards and gardens end up in our drinking water, which means we are also consuming them. These chemicals are so pervasive that polar bears—a remote, isolated species—show pesticides in their body fat.

IS MY BOTTLED WATER SAFE?

There is no way to circumvent water contamination, because bottled water comes from the same primary water sources as our drinking water. Approximately half of the US population drinks bottled water, and many people drink it on a regular basis. But does this mean the water is any safer? The answer is a resounding "no." The truth is that the government requirements for bottled water are more lax than those for tap water. Advertisements on bottled water imply the water is pristine and sourced from mountaintops or deep-well springs, but the cold truth is that bottled-water companies can (and do) use water from the tap as well as other treated and untreated sources. And bottled water companies do not have to disclose the source of their water or the results of the battery tests performed on it like tap water providers do. Bottled water can be treated or untreated water.

The Environmental Working Group, an environmental health and research advocacy organization, say they've found a broad range of contaminants—including pesticides, prescription medicines, industrial contaminants, heavy metals, and bacteria—in bottled water. They recommend filtered tap water as the safest choice for drinking water.[3] The Natural Resources Defense Council (NRDC), an environmental action group, found volatile organic chemicals in a significant number of samples tested that could cause cancer or disrupt the endocrine system. One of the worst incidences of contamination the NRDC found was that of one bottled water company (with several brands) whose well was located in the parking lot of an industrial warehouse near a state-designated hazardous waste site. Several chemicals with the potential to cause cancer and endocrine disruption were found in the bottled water that came from this site.[4]

Bottled water also has two other known problems as compared with tap water: it is stored in plastic bottles that can leach contaminants into the water, particularly if they are stored for a prolonged time in hot weather; and after we have consumed the water, the bottles contribute to the waste stream. Even if these bottles are recycled, a lot of energy is expended making and transporting them. Bottled water is a healthier choice than soda from a vending machine, but it does not effectively protect us from exposure to small amounts of chemical contaminants.

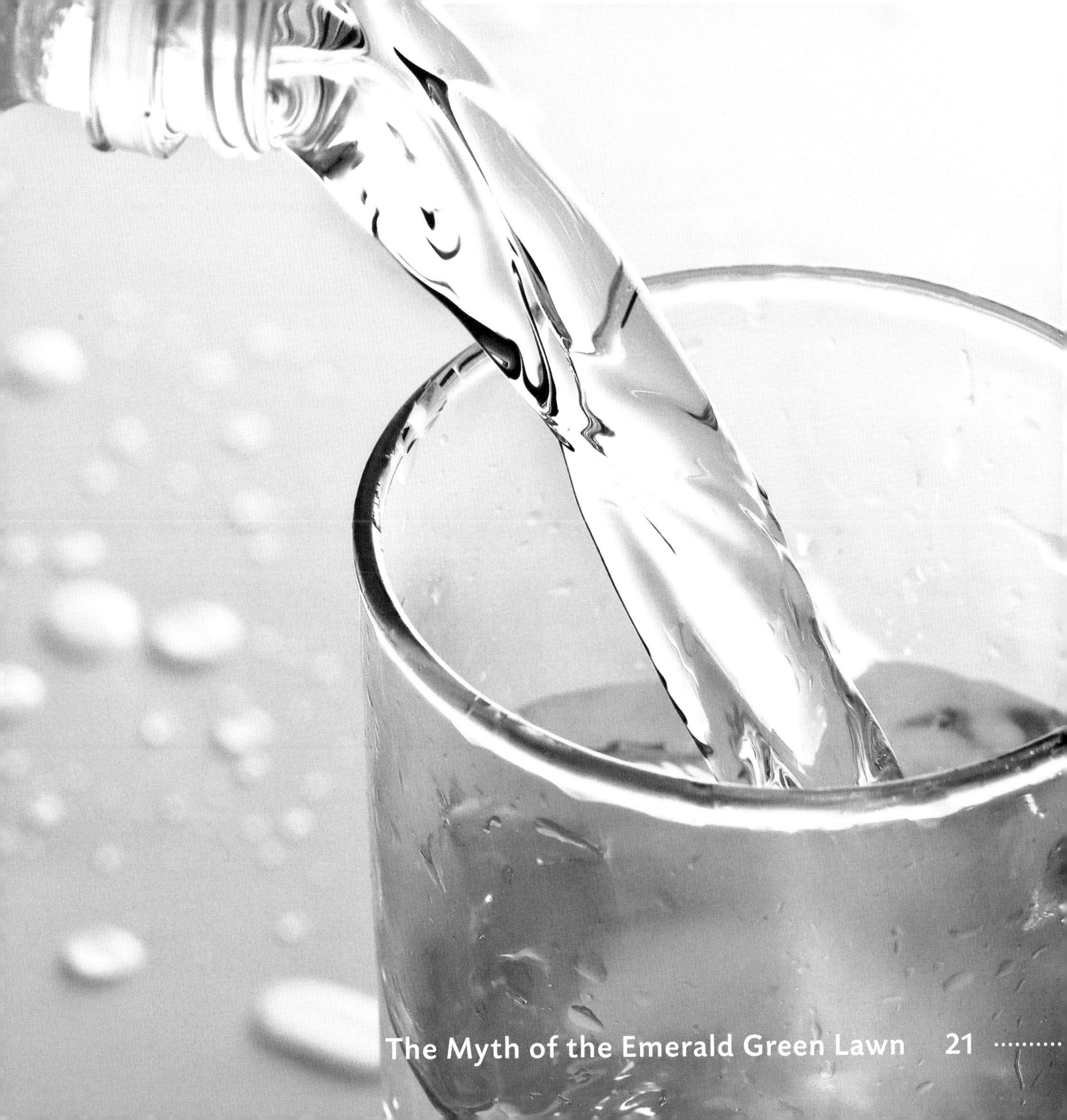

It's not difficult to imagine how these chemicals end up in our water supply, our bodies, and the bodies of remote species. 95 percent of the contiguous United States is directly impacted by how we care for our yards. While 41 percent of the land is devoted to agriculture, 54 percent is comprised of cities and suburbs.[5] This means homeowners are caring for most of the land in the United States. And every year, Americans use a staggering 80 million pounds of pesticide on 30 million acres of lawn—ten times more chemicals per acre than farmers use.[6] We would never intentionally put these chemicals into our children's drinking water, but, in effect, this is what we are doing. And because we can't see them, most of us are unaware they are there. Many of the yard chemicals that enter the water cycle do not degrade; instead, they accumulate in the environment. This not only puts our families but also generations to come at risk. Better

understanding their effects on our health is the most compelling reason for change, but understanding their origin is equally important.

HISTORY OF LAWN & GARDEN CHEMICALS

In general, we are more conscious of the effects of large-scale, toxic exposure on the body (such as in the stories portrayed in movies such as Silkwood or Erin Brockovich) than we are of the significance of exposure to everyday chemicals. 80,000 chemicals initially thought to be safe have been introduced into the market since World War II. Lawn and garden chemicals entered our environment en masse in the 1950s. Many of the chemicals we still use on our lawns and in our gardens (and their predecessors) were developed during World War II.[7] At that time, they were a veritable godsend, saving countless lives. The pesticides developed eradicated malaria-infected mosquitoes, protecting both soldiers and civilians. Synthetic fertilizers fueled an increase in crop production essential to winning the war, allowing the United States to feed its troops and also much of Europe during World War II. This economic demand fostered scientific inquiry and a staggering number of new chemicals were developed.

Corporations heavily invested in developing pesticides and fertilizers during World War II, and with the end of the war, they needed a new market. As countless GIs returned home, married, and purchased homes with yards, corporations had a new target market for their products. The companies marketed to men and played on their inherent competitiveness. Challenging men to have a better lawn than their neighbors was an effective strategy, and lawn care came to be thought of as a macho endeavor. An emerald green, dandelion-free lawn was marketed as an emblem of success. At the time it was believed that these pesticides and weed killers only hurt insects and plants and any exposure people received was insignificant. Likewise, fertilizers were thought to be safe, at least in small amounts.

Yard competition among neighbors was friendly and congenial. But in the 1970s, this target market began having children and worrisome trends developed, with this generation experiencing a dramatic rise in many of the diseases that can be caused by chemicals that disrupt our endocrine or hormonal systems. Figuratively, we discovered a snake in the grass.

Since the 1950s, progress has been made protecting Americans from large-scale industrial pollution. The Clean Water Act, passed in 1972 and amended to be more stringent in the 1980s, aims to prevent the release of toxic substances into water from industry, agriculture, and municipalities. Surprisingly, as industrial usage has become better regulated, one of the most significant sources of constant chemical exposure has become the ever-increasing amount of synthetic chemicals we use in our yards and gardens. And when we use these chemicals in our own yards, they don't just affect us through our drinking water—we breathe them in as air blows through our windows and absorb them through the skin as we walk on our lawns, and even pets track them into the house. A 2008 study showed that household dogs transported diazinon from lawns into homes and onto occupants. The study also showed that occupants were exposed through airborne dust particles and soil and had elevated diazinon urine levels. Even after eight days, diazinon levels were still elevated.[8]

HOW IS OUR HEALTH AT RISK?

Scientists used to believe small exposure to lawn and garden chemicals was safe. Now we know, mostly through hindsight, that even small exposure has serious health consequences. Many lawn and garden chemicals are comprised of substances that are known to be potential cancer-causing agents or "carcinogens," a term most of us are familiar with. Very small amounts of these chemicals were thought to be below a threshold that could cause cancer. But many chemicals in pesticides, weed killers, and fertilizers also harm us in a newly discovered and less familiar manner called endocrine disruption. Even in very, very small doses once thought to be safe, endocrine disruptors wreak havoc on our bodies by either blocking hormone function or mimick-

ing it. Hormones are responsible for many body functions, and disease can easily occur when hormone function is impaired. Most concerning is that research shows it's our children who are at greatest risk from exposure.

Considering the important role hormones play in our development, it isn't hard to imagine the impact endocrine disruptors have on a developing child. Exposure during development can have lifelong consequences. Endocrine disruptors have been linked to a long list of diseases, including abnormal brain and nervous-system development (leading to ADD, ADHD, autism, and intellectual impairment), as well as obesity, diabetes, and even cancer.[9][10][11][12][13] While children are most susceptible, adults are also affected, and these chemicals are thought to be contributing to the increasing rates of infertility, breast and prostate cancer, and adult onset diabetes.[14][15][16][17][18] Again, when we started using these chemicals freely in our everyday lives, we

FEDERAL DRINKING WATER STANDARDS

D rinking water standards are set by the United States Environmental Protection Agency, or EPA. A quick look at the agency's website on water protection is sobering. The website is geared toward water protection, but many links and studies on the website show just how at risk we are. The EPA is responsible for developing the National Primary Drinking Water Regulations, which set enforceable limits for more than ninety contaminants that may be found in public drinking water supplies. Regulated contaminants include several disease-causing microorganisms that can enter the water supply when it is contaminated by human or animal waste. The list also contains radionuclides, the disinfectants used in treating water, byproducts of disinfection, and organic and inorganic chemicals. Runoff from pesticides, weed killers, and fertilizers are among those inorganic and organic chemicals on the watchlist. The EPA also has a non-enforceable secondary list, and a list of chemicals that pose concern and need more investigation.[19] [20]

These regulations are partially developed based on what our water can actually achieve—meaning, our water will always suffer some degree of contamination, but there are acceptable exposure limits not thought to have a large risk of harming a person's health. The task is daunting, constantly evolving, and needs to take into account the incidence of contamination, cost and feasibility of testing, and potential harm caused to the population by specific exposures. Tests corroborating the risk of a chemical need to be proven and standardized, and tests for endocrine disruptors are just now being developed. Short and long-term health exposure effects are detailed on the regulation list and range from risk of cancer, thyroid disease, and kidney problems to intestinal, liver, and reproductive problems, among many others.

As mentioned previously, what these lists do not take into account is that many endocrine-disrupting chemicals and pharmaceutical residues can act cumulatively, so individual exposure risk is greater. For example, studies have shown that young girls exposed to high levels of estrogen mimics can experience early-onset puberty, and in fact the age that most girls can expect to experience puberty has gotten lower and lower over the past fifty years.[21] So while individual pesticide, weed killer, and fertilizer contamination may be within federal regulatory limits, they still pose a significant health threat because we are exposed to the estrogen-mimicking chemicals from all of these substances combined. This is problematic, and the EPA notes this limitation of its current testing and regulatory procedures on its website. In the case of pharmaceutical residues, it's easy to comprehend why drinking small amounts of birth control pills, antidepressants, pain medicine, and che-

motherapy drugs is not a good idea. All of these exposures add up.

The task of protecting our water and keeping it free of pollutants is difficult. The EPA and large cities like New York have realized it's not possible or economical to remove all of these contaminants from drinking water supplies, but also understand that these chemicals pose a significant threat to the population. Because of this, and given the enormity of the task of ensuring water quality, much of the EPA website is focused on prevention and what citizens and communities can do to protect water. The EPA does work with state agencies to enforce water quality. However, water treatment is never perfect, and protecting the quality of our water means not introducing chemicals into the water. This means that keeping our water safe and healthy isn't any one person's or agency's responsibility—it's all of our responsibility.

didn't know such small amounts were dangerous. Also, the US population has grown and we are using more chemicals now than ever, increasing our exposure and risk. These chemicals are much more damaging than we once thought.

ANCILLARY THREATS TO OUR HEALTH & WATER

Though not the focus of this book, it is worth mentioning two other significant threats to our health and water supply:

- Pharmaceutical drugs
- Household cleaning products

These products act on our water in a couple of ways when they are flushed or disposed of down the drain. Like lawn and garden chemicals, these products contain compounds that do not break down in the water cycle and therefore end up in the water supply. And we've generally talked about how all these chemicals prey upon our health. But pharmaceutical drugs and household cleaners can also harm the function of septic systems, used by many homes in the United States to treat waste, by killing off important bacteria necessary for waste breakdown or by creating inhospitable conditions for these bacteria to thrive. If there are no bacteria present to break down waste where septic systems are in use, we run the risk of sewage contaminating the water supply as well—again, affecting our health.

Pharmaceuticals

According to the US Geological Survey (USGS), pharmaceutical drugs are frequently detected in ground and untreated drinking water sources. Some are carcinogens and some are endocrine disruptors. In 2008, the USGS conducted a study to determine the extent of pharmaceutical and other organic wastewater contaminants (OWCs) in our water. 81 percent of the groundwater samples tested positive for contamination by drugs and household chemicals that were disposed of into septic systems.[22] Another study revealed that several hormones and antibiotics originating from septic systems were found in measurable amounts in ponds and lakes after groundwater contaminated by the septic systems mixed with those water bodies.

In a 2004 study, the USGS, in conjunction with the Center for Disease Control, tested a drinking water treatment plant to determine whether pharmaceuticals and other OWCs persisted after treatment.[23] They found that many did, but at levels within Federal Drinking Water Standards. They noted, however, that these standards are for individual contaminants and are not based on the combined effect of all of the contaminants—and that these contaminants may act cumulatively on a person's health. In other words, if several of the contaminants in a glass of drinking water are estrogen mimics, the to-tal estrogenic exposure is much higher than the exposure a person would experience if there was only one estrogen mimic involved.[24] [25] [26] [27]

Household Cleaners

Many household cleaners don't list ingredients on the containers, and while we only use small amounts of these products day to day, the amount of product used over many years adds up. Flushing or pouring household cleaners down the drain can impact water quality in two ways. First, some of the chemical compounds found in cleaners—which may contain carcinogens or endocrine disruptors—don't get filtered out in the water cycle and also do not degrade. Second, when these chemicals enter septic systems, they kill bacteria in the septic system crucial to the breakdown of waste. For most of the cleaners we use in our homes there are commercial or homemade alternatives that are water quality-friendly.

SOLD ON GREEN: THE LAWN & GARDEN INDUSTRY AND ADVERTISING

As we learned earlier, the emerald green lawn reached iconic status after World War II, when the burgeoning lawn and garden industry directed its advertising and marketing at returning GIs settling into new homes. Today, the US lawn and garden industry is a billion-dollar industry that spends millions on advertising.

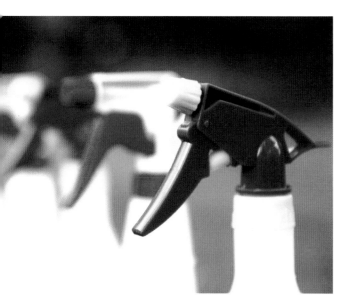

Most of us feel that we can look past the bias in advertising and sift out the facts. Madison Avenue knows this isn't true. Those who work in advertising make the study of human behavior their business. They understand consumers better than consumers understand themselves. Advertising is so pervasive these days that none of us are immune to its reach—so pervasive, in fact, that the Bureau of Consumer Protection of the Federal Trade Commission has sponsored an initiative to educate children on how advertising works so they can better navigate the choices in the very commercial world into which they've been born.

When we hear lawn and garden ads on the radio, they often target men, appealing to their machismo or desire to one-up their neighbor. When we see lawn and garden ads on TV, men and women are being sold a lifestyle—one that they want, with happy, smiling children and puppies playing on beautifully manicured lawns. The message is simple: purchase these lawn and garden products and this will be your life. But the reality of most of these lawn and garden products is quite different: they are toxic to you, your family, and your pets, and they end up in the water supply.

The lawn and garden industry is projected to see growth in the coming years as the economy recovers and people buy real estate and install lawns and gardens. Sales for pesticides and fertilizers are projected to increase and remain high.[28] The positive news is that with growing environmental awareness, the upswing in lawn and garden consumables will be accompanied by a demand for more environmentally friendly products.

THE GREAT HEALTHY YARD PROJECT— A SIMPLE SOLUTION

Protecting our families' health and improving our water quality is simple. If we practice Minimal Impact Management—do not use chemicals in our yards and gardens, and don't dispose of pharmaceuticals and cleaning products down our drains—we won't put our families at risk and our water quality will improve.

It really is this simple.

Homeowners are caring for most of the land in the United States, which means small changes can make a huge impact. Changing our behavior is the fastest way to improve water quality and decrease our health risk. Understanding that the chemicals we put in our yards and gardens end up in our drinking water is our incentive. Taking care of our yards is taking care of our water. And this doesn't mean our yards have to be "certified organic." Again, this book is not about absolutes—it's about making small, constructive changes every day.

What is Minimal Impact Management?

Minimal Impact Design (MID) or Low Impact Design (LID) are terms used in reference to storm water management. As we will cover more in-depth in the next chapter, storm water is a threat to our water because it washes surface toxins and debris into our drinking water sources and can flood wastewater treatment plants, resulting in the release of untreated waste from these sources as well. As a preventive measure, many communities have developed MID or LID plans to minimize the impact of storm water on our drinking water—planting green infrastructure trees, and creating catch basins, rain gardens, and other thoughtful designs that channel rain water so it can be absorbed close to where it falls and does not enter the storm water flow. Essentially, these plans aim to work with an area's natural hydrology to minimize pollution entering the sources of our drinking water.

For the purposes of The Great Healthy Yard Project, however, we use the term Minimal Impact Management (rather than design) as a plan for protecting our water supply by managing our homes, yards, and gardens with the least tox-ic footprint possible. This means not disposing of household cleaners down the drain or flushing unwanted pharmaceutical drugs. This means refraining from the use of synthetic chemicals—pesticides, weed killers, or fertilizers—on our lawns and in our gardens, since we know these chemicals wash into our water supply. It also means planting native plants, trees, and shrubs to absorb and filter storm water as well as support native wildlife. Minimal Impact Management can also mean minimal, localized use of pesticides or weed killers to resolve an infestation or improve habitat for native plants and wildlife crucial for water quality, or to eradicate invasive species, which can harm the water supply in a number of ways. Fortunately, caring for our yards without synthetic chemicals isn't time-consuming or expensive. In fact, it often saves money that would be spent on chemical treatments.

Yards can flourish without synthetic chemical use.

But even more important than a beautiful yard is understanding the true impact of pesticides, weed killers, and fertilizers on our health, water quality, and community. All change first requires impetus. The Great Healthy Yard Project will provide this by exploring:

- How pesticides, weed killers, and fertilizers enter the water cycle
- How pesticides, weed killers, and fertilizers affect the human body
- How to improve water quality through alternative lawn and garden care

Though change is one of the most difficult things for people to embrace, once we have this understanding, we are not only obligated to act—we want to. After all, our children's health is at stake. How we garden is important. Water is a shared, life-sustaining resource. As more people adopt Minimal Impact Management, we will see a drastic improvement in our water supply. It is the hope of The Great Healthy Yard Project that your new understanding will compel you to share the information in this book to help further educate communities to work in protection of watersheds.

CHAPTER 2:

How Water Works

"When the well's dry, we know the worth of water."
—Benjamin Franklin (1706-1790), Poor Richard's Almanac, 1746

70 percent of the earth is covered in water. Our bodies are 60 percent water. Our blood is more than 80 percent water. "Water is life's mater and matrix, mother and medium," said Nobel Prize-winning biochemist Albert Szent-Gyorgyi. "There is no life without water." Yet how much do we really know about water—specifically, the water we use every day to bathe, clean, cook, and drink?

As we discussed in Chapter 1, many of the pollutants entering our water system are chemicals we use in our yards and households. To understand how pesticides, fertilizers, weed killers, pharmaceuticals, and household cleaners get into our drinking water, we have to look beyond the tap. These pollutants are not visible, so we're unaware of them, but when they enter our bodies with the water we drink they have serious consequences to our health.

To understand how to keep our drinking water clean, it's important to understand where our water comes from. For that we need to be familiar with the concepts of surface and groundwater, and what an aquifer and watershed area is. We also need to understand where our wastewater ends up. With the population of the United States reaching over 315 million in 2013, many of us are drinking it.

COMING TO TERMS WITH WATER

Water can be divided into several categories, and while the terms used to describe these categories may sound rather technical, understanding them is important to carrying on discussions about water: where it comes from, how it gets to us, how pollutants find their way to water sources, and what we can do to protect our water and, ultimately, our families.

Some terms are simple and based on usage. "Potable water" simply describes fresh water that is destined to be used for our drinking water. The word "potable" comes from the Latin word potare, which means "to drink." The term "wastewater" is pretty clear: this is water that has already been used and has waste products in it. Wastewater can be divided into "grey water" and "black water." Grey water is water that has been used for showering or dishes and can be reused for watering plants or flushing toilets. Black water contains human, animal, or industrial waste and needs to be treated before it re-enters the water cycle. Some private homes and commercial buildings separate the two so grey water can be reused in the house or garden or for other purposes. Other terms used to describe the water cycle are based on where water is as it passes through the cycle.

Following are a few more definitions to help you navigate the water cycle. These definitions will give you a better understanding of just how easy it is for dangerous chemicals to end up in the water supply.

Surface Water

When it rains, the water that is not absorbed into the ground runs downhill into streams, rivers, lakes, and reservoirs. These water bodies are called surface water. Most communities have their share of "impervious surfaces," such as roofs, sidewalks, and paved roads, where water cannot penetrate the ground. This water runs directly into wetlands, streams, lakes, and reservoirs, carrying toxic debris with it.

Storm Water

When rain or snow hits the ground we call it storm water because it's visible and has potential to cause

ONE BRYANT PARK

One Bryant Park in New York City became the first Leed Platinum Certified commercial skyscraper in the United States in 2010. One Bryant Park reuses treated grey water onsite for air conditioning. The tower also captures all rainwater that falls onsite, stores it, and uses it for flushing toilets and watering plants to decrease the building's water usage.

problems. Storm water naturally runs downward along the surface of the earth, from the highest to lowest point, pooling in streams and lakes and sometimes causing them to overflow. It carries with it organic debris from leaves and loose soil, causing erosion. This debris can cause excessive growth of algae in streams and lakes, sapping them of their oxygen and making conditions uninhabitable for fish. Storm water also carries any toxic chemicals we have used in our yards with it.

Groundwater

Groundwater is rainwater that is absorbed into the ground. During absorption, the water begins a natural filtering process and travels hundreds of feet down until it reaches underground streams called "aquifers." At this point it is dubbed "groundwater."

Aquifer

An aquifer is an underground stream or layer of water contained in porous rock. Most well water comes from aquifers that are hundreds of feet underground. Aquifers are tapped for drinking water.

Recharge

Recharge is a water cycle term that means the replacement or resupply of water. Groundwater aquifers are linked to underground streams, lakes, and reservoirs that recharge (mix with) them.

Drinking Water

Drinking water comes from groundwater or surface water. In many small communities, people drink untreated water from private or municipal groundwater wells. Surface water, however, is usually treated to remove contaminants such as parasites.

Water Table

A water table is defined as the depth below which the ground is saturated with water and is associated with an aquifer. The water table often rises near rivers and lakes.

Watershed

A watershed is an area where all water, both above and below ground, tends to pool in one place. A watershed can be the size of a neighborhood or large region.[29]

Reservoir

Reservoirs are manmade lakes that are used to capture surface water and control its distribution for drinking and irrigation. Reservoirs are usually constructed in areas that naturally fill from streams.

Septic System

A septic system is an individual wastewater treatment system and is commonly used in homes in small communities that lack the resources or the necessities for community sewage and wastewater treatment.

Wastewater Treatment Facility

A wastewater treatment facility is a plant designed to remove biological, chemical, and other contaminants from water before the water is discharged back into the water cycle. Components of this process usually include bacterial degradation, mechanical filtering, and the use of chlorine, chloramine, or ultraviolet light to kill bacteria, viruses, and parasites.

Though purification of water does occur as it is naturally filtered or treated through the drinking water cycle, a topic we'll explore shortly in this chapter, some pollutants are not getting filtered out—namely, small but significant amounts of lawn chemicals and pharmaceuticals.

Now that we are comfortable with the terms, let's briefly review what we know about the water cycle and drinking water's place within that cycle. Since this book is concerned with drinking water, we will only concern ourselves with freshwater sources.

THE DRINKING WATER CYCLE

Most of us learned about the water cycle in grade school, and though we don't think much about it on a day-to-day basis anymore, we do understand it in simple, sweeping terms. But how much do we know about where our drinking water fits into this cycle? And do we know what happens to water when it hits the earth's surface, and what processes then take place?

In a simplistic view, and with our new understanding of the related terms, water moves in a continual process, from clouds above the earth to the earth's surface (through rain), where it enters streams, rivers, and lakes. Streams, rivers, and lakes are considered surface water because they're on the earth's surface. Some water evaporates from these surface water sources, refueling the water cycle process. However, some rainwater is absorbed into the soil. This water travels deep below the earth and is called groundwater, because it enters the ground. Groundwater can travel in underground rivers, which usually move much more slowly than rivers above the surface because they move through porous rock. It can also be widely dispersed underground. Together, these sources of underground water are called aquifers. Groundwater can eventually flow into surface water bodies such as lakes or streams and recharge them. When they mix, groundwater carries minerals from rock and soil, as well as debris not filtered out through the natural process. Surface water contains plant and other debris that washes into it by storm or rainwater from impervious surfaces. Because surface water and groundwater mix, any contaminants in the water will also mix to some degree.[30]

Nature's Water Filters

Water that has been used by people and animals has always re-entered the water cycle, becoming drinking water once again. Natural filtering by soil, sand, and rock, as well as marshes and wetlands, once sufficed to maintain water quality, and it still does in small communities.

GROUNDWATER: SOIL, SAND & ROCK

Groundwater has several natural opportunities for purification, the first of which is absorption by soil bacteria and plants. Soil bacteria and plants absorb excess nutrients and pollutants (soil bacteria can even degrade some pollutants). Once through the soil, groundwater also benefits from being filtered by sand and fractured or porous rock: the pores in rock and sand trap substances. Dissolved substances not broken down by bacteria and smaller than the pores in the rock avoid trapping and end up in the groundwater. Groundwater is generally cleaner than surface water because of this filtering process. In general, groundwater does not contain parasites or bacteria unless a nearby septic system has polluted it; however, toxic chemicals do slip through its filtering system.

SURFACE WATER: MARSHES & WETLANDS

Marshes and wetlands are nature's way of cleaning surface water. Marshes are mostly made up of surface water, and they serve as sponges that absorb excess water during storms and help prevent flooding. Marshes naturally filter surface water before it enters nearby streams, rivers, and lakes: their verdant plant life, such as cattails and water lilies, absorb some excess nutrients and pollutants, and their beneficial soil bacteria degrade some pollutants.

Manmade Filtration Systems: Drinking Water Treatment Plants

Municipalities and cities use water treatment facilities to process wastewater and purify drinking water for the community, though small communities may adopt one or more of the basic tenets of a water treatment facility, outlined here. It's easy to find out which (if any) of these processes are used in your community.

STEP 1: COAGULATION

In the coagulation process—so named because the material used clumps like a blood clot—sticky particles are added that particulate impurities in the water will cling to. Aluminum and iron salts are commonly used to attract impurities. Some systems use synthetic molecules, too. These sticky substances are called "floc." When floc and impurities combine, they sink to the bottom.

STEP 2: SEDIMENTATION

As the floc and impurities settle to the bottom, the water moves through a pipe to the next stage, leaving the clumped debris behind.

STEP 3: FILTRATION

Sand, clay, or charcoal filters are used to filter the water. These filters remove molecules that fit into their pores. Molecules that are smaller than the pores in the filter, including some toxic chemicals, pass through with the water.

STEP 4: DISINFECTION

After filtration, the water is often disinfected with either chlorine or chloramine. Ultraviolet light further disinfects the water, killing parasites. Ozination

is sometimes used as a disinfectant. Ozone is an oxidizing agent that readily gives up an oxygen molecule and kills bacteria, viruses, and parasites.

SMALL-TOWN & BIG-CITY DRINKING WATER

Perhaps the best approach to understanding drinking water and its cycle is to look at both contemporary and historical examples of how small and large communities handle issues around drinking water. Small communities usually have a much different relationship with water than cities do. This is partly because they're directly responsible for their water quality and have limited resources to deal with water quality issues. Since it's much cheaper to take preventive measures with water quality than treat it, small communities are often vigilant about their water. Today, large cities, such as New York, are also learning that it's financially more effective to prevent pollutants from entering the water in the first place rather than trying to remove them, even if the watershed is large and at a great distance from the city.

In this section we will explore the drinking water process for both small communities and large cities. We will begin by looking at the small community of Bedford, New York, since understanding where we get our drinking water in small communities makes it easier to understand how water works in large cities. Following small communities, we'll take a look at a large city—New York City. And the ties between Bedford and New York City's drinking water go deep.

Case History: Drinking Water in a Small Town

Bedford, New York is a town of 16,000 people located forty-eight miles north of New York City. Unlike a city—where both the source of the water and the waste are often out of sight and out of mind—Bedford is dependent on wells and

HETCH HETCHY

ince population density and concomitant waste often make it necessary for large cities to obtain their drinking water from distant, less-populated and more pristine areas, the sometimes large-scale threats to city water can seem distant, too, unless there is a calamity that brings the threat close to home. The recent California Rim Fire threatening Yosemite National Park brought the mental disconnect regarding where cities obtain their water to national attention. As the fire threatened Yosemite, many were surprised that a state of emergency was called in San Francisco. Much of the country, including many San Francisco residents, learned for the first time that San Francisco obtains 85 percent of its water from the Hetch Hetchy reservoir, which is 150 miles away from the city. Heavy ash contamination threatened this water system.[31]

septic systems, and residents are aware that their actions directly affect the water quality.

Like many other communities, the three downtown hamlets in Bedford—Katonah, Bedford Hills, and Bedford—were developed over a century ago, when the population was much smaller and when knowledge of how to maintain water quality was much less advanced. The history of Katonah is perhaps most deeply intertwined with the history of water use in the Hudson Valley. In the mid-1800s, Old Katonah was located just east of the railroad tracks used to bring fresh milk into New York City from local dairy farms. The farms were clustered around the Cross River, which provided ample water for the residents, their fields, and their livestock. This water was not only precious to local farmers but also to the growing city, only an hour's train ride south.

In 1890, New York City began proceedings to take possession of the town by eminent domain and flood it to create one of the reservoirs in a system that would bring fresh water into the city. Residents fought the city in court, but the city prevailed. While other towns that were commandeered usually disbanded, Katonah was tightly knit and wanted to remain a community. Residents formed the Katonah Land Company and purchased land on the west side of the railroad tracks. They hired architects B.S. and G.S. Olmsted, who planned a Victorian community in the shape of a cross one mile south of Old Katonah. In 1897, residents began moving their homes on logs pulled by teams of horses to the new town.[32]

The new town of Katonah had an ample water supply because it was built directly over a very large aquifer. Today this aquifer not only supplies local groundwater wells, but also feeds into the adjacent Muscoot Reservoir, which serves New York City. Current planning standards would call for development far from the aquifer to protect it from contaminants, but in

1897, quantity was the concern and long-term quality was taken for granted.

The population of Bedford has increased dramatically over the years, as has the number of visitors to stores and restaurants in town. Because of this increase in population and development, Bedford has faced threats to its local water quality. In the 1980s, several wells were contaminated with dry-cleaning fluid, leading to the creation of a Superfund Water District. This demonstrates that even suburban areas with no heavy industry can become contaminated with industrial pollutants, and these pollutants travel into our groundwater in the same way that lawn chemicals do: they are absorbed into the ground with rainwater and eventually reach the drinking water aquifer. Bedford also saw household wells adjacent to a golf course in a neighboring town become polluted when pesticides were accidentally spilled and the contents washed into the groundwater aquifer.

In order to ensure a long-term supply of fresh, potable water to the hamlets of Katonah and Bedford Hills, where population density is highest and the risk for nitrate pollution from septic systems the greatest, Bedford has just tapped into one of New York City's major aqueducts, which passes under the town. While New York City drinking water remains unfiltered, the city requires towns that tap into its aqueduct to filter the water. The biggest concerns, both in reservoirs and in the streams and rivers of the Catskills, are Giardia and Cryptosporidia from animal waste. The water is chlorinated after it is filtered to kill bacteria, viruses, and parasites. The filters need to be cleaned with chlorine, too, so they do not accumulate bacteria. This means that the filtrate—the semi-solid material that does not pass through the filter and has been separated from the drinking water—contains chlorinated hydrocarbons that can be both carcinogens and endocrine disruptors. This waste is trucked to the sewage treatment facility at Bedford Hills Correctional Facility. While it is greatly improved after treatment, the process does not remove all of the chemicals from the water, which is discharged with the rest of the treated wastewater from the facility into a stream that drains into New York City's Muscoot Reservoir.

While this process alleviates one problem, nitrate pollution, it poses another. Because the watershed for the downtown hamlets is now distant, Bedford, along with New York City, faces the threats posed by how distant communities behave in what is now a shared watershed. This includes not only lawn chemicals used by upstate residents that enter the watershed by absorption into groundwater and wash with storm water runoff into streams and lakes upstate but also pharmaceuticals and cleaning products that are disposed of down the drain by upstate residents and hospitals.

In Bedford, there is no centralized sewer system or sewage treatment facility. This can be seen, in some respects, as protecting the town from development. With increased development in communities that rely on septic systems, there is often a concomitant increase in pollution of the groundwater. Because the waste is not transported to a sewage treatment facility, either in the town or out of it, the filtering capability of the soil can be overwhelmed, and nitrates from the waste end up in the aquifer if there are too many septic systems.

Strict septic ordinances and monitoring of industries can combat this issue, but ultimately, towns that do not pump their sewage out of town—and that rely on local water, as Bedford does—must limit development or risk groundwater contamination. Bedford thus has strict building codes limiting impervious surfaces and maintaining adequate separation of septic systems. Bedford does not allow building on steep slopes because of runoff, and it protects its wetlands and trees, because they filter water. No fertilizer or pesticide application is allowed in wetland areas since, once dissolved, they travel with the water into streams and ponds or are absorbed into the aquifer. Bedford also now works closely with the two golf courses in town on prevention. These courses have developed best practices to limit pesticide usage, preventing spills and waste from entering the groundwater and wetlands.

SEPTIC SYSTEMS IN SMALL COMMUNITIES

A conventional septic system consists of a waste pipe that leaves the house and enters a storage tank where solid waste settles and is stored and liquefied by bacteria. The bacteria that degrade the waste in the tank need air and also nutrients from the waste in order to grow. An average residential septic tank holds about 1,500 gallons, and the average individual uses about 100 gallons of water a day. So if only one person is residing in the residence, the tank is filled in less than three weeks. Routine pumping of the tank, usually every two to three years, removes any excess debris and maintains room at the bottom of the tank for settling and air at the top of the tank to support the bacteria necessary for degradation. The resulting liquid then exits the tank by a pipe and is distributed over a leaching field, where it is degraded by soil bacteria and filtered by rock and sand as it slowly absorbs hundreds of feet down into the aquifer.

Well-made septic systems trap wastewater and allow bacteria and soil to filter it before it reaches the aquifer. If, however, the septic system is not well maintained, not of an adequate size for the amount of discharge, or clogged, or if the soil is not porous, then it fails. In this case, wastewater joins with rainwater and runs into streams, rivers, and lakes, without filtering, and pollutes them. When this happens, nitrates and E. coli bacteria end up in lakes and streams. When a septic system is functioning well, however, soil bacteria take urea from the waste and convert it into nitrate and ammonia, which plants can use. Excess nitrogen can also pollute the groundwater aquifer. If the source of pollution is removed, the aquifer will eventually dilute out the pollutant and replenish itself, but this can take a long time, and some toxic chemicals do not degrade.

Some small communities have small wastewater treatment facilities or advanced septic

technologies to process waste in downtown areas or from schools or businesses. While septic systems release waste into leaching fields, which means it is naturally filtered before it reaches groundwater, these wastewater treatment facilities may either leach the waste into fields or discharge liquid waste into streams or lakes. Waste discharged into streams and lakes is usually required to be treated more fully than leached waste, since there are no soil bacteria to degrade the pollutants or rocks to filter them. In these cases, filtering and ultraviolet light are usually required to kill bacteria and parasites. This process is important so our streams, rivers, and lakes can support wildlife, which, in turn, support the quality of our drinking water.

Pharmaceutical Drugs & Cleaning Products

Pharmaceutical drugs and household cleaning agents also pose risks to septic system maintenance. Both destroy conditions for the necessary bacteria in the septic system, which poses two problems: the septic system can't provide its function, and both toxic chemicals and sub-optimally treated wastewater penetrate the soil and contaminate the groundwater. As we learned earlier, groundwater and surface water eventually recharge (mix), so these chemicals find their way into streams and reservoirs. Bacterial degradation and filtering by porous rock destroys or filters out some chemicals, but not all of them.

TO RECAP: HOW BEDFORD PROTECTS ITS DRINKING WATER

- Laws protecting wetlands and wetland buffers
- Prohibits use of pesticides and fertilizers in wetland areas and buffers
- Maintains "steep slope" legislation to avoid storm water runoff
- Limits impervious or impermeable surface building
- Requires all septic systems pumped and inspected every five years
- Limits water usage for businesses where septic systems are close together
- Maintains and adds catch basins to hold and filter storm water
- Protects trees
- Plants rain gardens and street trees
- Plants trees in non-forested riparian areas
- Requires adequate spacing between wells and new septic systems
- Requires all homes sold to have wells tested prior to sale

Case History: Drinking Water in a Big City

New York City was settled by Europeans in the 1600s. Water initially came from local wells, ponds, and springs. The population outgrew its supply eventually, which led to uncontrolled fires. In addition, much of the drinking water was contaminated

HYDROFRACKING

The desire for energy independence from Middle East oil, compounded with the poor economy and a governor with political ambitions, has put New York in the spotlight as energy companies seek permits to drill for natural gas in the Marcellus Shale of upstate New York. The Marcellus Shale is a rock formation that stretches across West Virginia, Ohio, Pennsylvania, and New York.

Drilling for natural gas is accomplished through a process called "hydrofracking," a new drilling technique that allows gas to be extracted from wells that were too deep to be economically viable sources in the past. To start, a large amount of water is removed from the ground. This water is then mixed with chemicals and sand and blasted under pressure with the drilling process to release natural gas from the pores in the rock. Chemicals are mixed with the water to lubricate it and prevent corrosion of drilling equipment.

Hydrofracking requires proprietary chemicals, 350 of which are publicly disclosed.[33] Companies will not reveal, however, which of the 350 chemicals will be used, claiming competitive corporate privacy. Hydrofracking creates a huge amount of wastewater containing these undisclosed chemicals, and also heavy metals and NORMs (normally occurring radioactive materials) present in the shale. These heavy metals and NORMs are not dangerous until hydrofracking brings them into contact with people and the water supply.

Water pollution near hydrofracking sites is common.[34] Faucets can ignite because of the methane gas that has escaped into the aquifer during drilling, and the water becomes turbid and foul from these pollutants. If these drilling permits are granted, it is likely that local wells in upstate New York will be polluted, as might the water going into the Delaware Aqueduct. This would pollute the water supply for Bedford—and for all New York City. New York State is planning to require setbacks of 1,000 feet from the boundaries of the New York City watershed. The process will likely infringe on the watershed, deep below the surface.

with human waste. Beer became the drink of choice since the water in beer was purified during distillation, preventing disease. Finally, in 1832, there was a cholera epidemic that killed 3,500 people, forcing the city to redouble its efforts to secure an adequate supply of fresh drinking water.

New York City looked north to less heavily populated areas in hopes that the water there was not polluted. In 1837, construction began on the Croton Aqueduct to bring water from Westchester County, about 60 miles north of the city, to New York City. Water from Westchester County first flowed into the city in 1842. In response to continued growing need, the City subsequently looked 130 miles north to the Catskill region for water. The Catskill reservoirs and aqueducts were developed in 1927, and the Delaware reservoirs and aqueducts, also from the Catskill area, were developed by 1945.[35] [36]

The aqueduct tunnels that transport New York City's water are made from concrete and have been reinforced with steel over the years in a few places where the surrounding rock is susceptible to movement. The tunnels vary in width from about a foot in diameter to just under 20 feet, and are located as deep as 150 to 1,500 feet beneath the ground. Both the Catskill and the Delaware aqueducts carry about half a billion gallons of water each to New York City every day. The City has been aware of a leak in the Delaware Aqueduct since the late 1980s that allows millions of gallons of water to escape every day in an upstate area where it passes through fragile limestone that has moved and cracked. Leaks not only waste precious drinking water and saturate areas that shouldn't be wet, but are also potential inroads for contamination. New York City is planning to build a three-mile bypass tunnel, at a cost of over a billion dollars, to divert the water around the leak while they fix it.[37]

To put this in perspective, the Delaware Aqueduct alone is 85 miles long and the Catskill Aqueduct is 163 miles long. Just to get the water

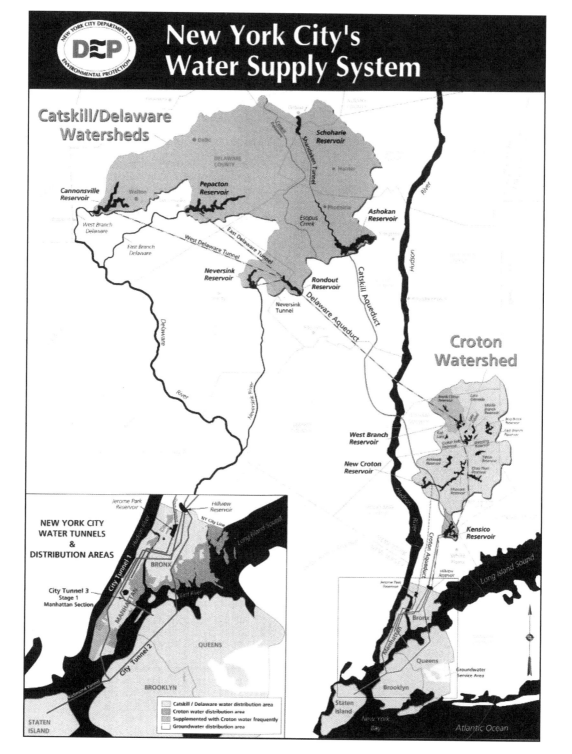

to the city requires three upstate reservoir systems consisting of nineteen reservoirs and three controlled lakes. Upkeep is a huge issue. When the leak to the Delaware Aqueduct is bypassed, towns below the bypass that depend on the aqueduct for water will need a water supply. To accomplish this, the city is building an upstate connection between the Catskill and Delaware aqueducts. This will also give the city some flexibility in their water supply in the future.

New York City has the largest unfiltered drinking water system in the nation, using over a billion gallons of water a day. Filtering over a billion gallons of water a day would be cost-prohibitive, so New York City works instead to protect its upstate watersheds. In fact, 10 percent of the city's water comes from the more densely populated Croton Watershed, which is located east of the Hudson River. In the 1990s, the EPA decided that since the population in this region is denser, the water requires filtering. New York

City is building a 3 billion-dollar plant in the Bronx to treat this small portion of its supply.[38]

New York City's drinking water is a surface water supply that comes from lakes and streams in its upstate watersheds. Because residents in the city do not live near their watershed, they do not have direct control of their drinking water. Many residents picture their drinking water coming from pristine mountains where rainwater and snow melt cascade down untouched, rocky slopes. While this is still true in some areas, there are now communities inhabiting much of the watershed. How people maintain their yards and gardens in Delaware, Greene, Sullivan, Schoharie, and Ulster Counties, home to the Catskill and Delaware Aqueducts, affects not only the water quality in those communities but also the water quality in the Catskill and Delaware Aqueducts, as well as the homes of people in New York City. In this sense, New York City's watershed is a compilation of watersheds of small communities. Implementing strategies discussed in the section on small communities in these upstate towns is a large component of maintaining New York City's water quality.

All drinking water in New York City is chlorinated. Due to concerns about parasites such as Giardia, the city is currently building the Catskill-Delaware Water Ultraviolet Disinfection Facility in Westchester County for additional disinfection. Overall, New York City has found that it is more cost-effective to buy and protect land in the watershed, especially west of the Hudson (the Catskill and Delaware watersheds) where the land is cheaper, than it is to treat sullied water. The New York City Department of Environmental Protection's Land Acquisition Program has purchased or conserved over 70,000 acres west of the Hudson since its inception in 1997.[39] In addition, to facilitate protection of its upstate watershed, New York City signed a watershed agreement with local towns in 1997. This agreement creates a collaborative partnership between New York City and watershed towns to protect the water. New York City also helps schools and communities install or update small treatment plants to maintain the quality of water being discharged into streams or lakes that lead into the city's reservoirs.[40]

TO RECAP: HOW NEW YORK CITY PROTECTS ITS DRINKING WATER

- Storm water management
- Wastewater treatment plant upgrades
- Septic system repairs and replacement
- Forestry
- Nonpoint source pollution control and management
- Land acquisition
- Stream and wetland disturbance monitoring
- Separating municipal sewers from storm water
- Pharmaceutical monitoring

In this chapter we have seen that skyrocketing populations and increasing demands on limited resources have placed our wastewater much closer to our drinking water. We have also seen how both small towns and big cities face local and distant threats to their water supplies. Small communities generally face local threats such as ill-maintained septic systems, chemical leaks, or weather-related disasters. Threats to big-city water supplies are often "out of sight," since most big cities obtain their water from a distance. Because of this, big cities rely on, and often partner with, small communities living in the area of their water supply to keep the water fresh and free from contamination. And both big and small communities take a variety of measures to protect their water. However, both are coming to realize through recent research that despite best efforts, some toxic chemicals pass through all stages of filtration—and one of the biggest threats comes from our own backyards.

It really is this simple: the toxic products we use in our yards and put down our drains end up in our water supply.

As we have learned, these chemicals are found even in isolated places and species like the polar bear. Many of these chemicals are resistant to degradation. Most worrisome, however, is the toxic effect they have on our bodies, even in small amounts. In Chapter 3, we will take a close look at the everyday chemicals people use in and around their homes and the recent medical research on their side effects. You will learn that those most at risk for developing serious problems from these chemicals are our children and people with genetic predispositions to certain illnesses.

CHAPTER 3:

How Toxic Chemicals Put Us At Risk

"Every human being is the author of his own health or disease."
—Buddha

Now that we have a basic understanding of how water works, we know that when we use lawn and garden chemicals, or put household cleaning products or pharmaceuticals down the drain, they travel with rainwater to our water sources and pollute them. When we ingest sullied water, these chemicals store themselves in our bodies and blood. Most of us understand that ingesting chemicals is not good for our health. But most of us don't know the actual effect of these chemicals on the body. Since we ingest only small amounts of them—and because we don't see, smell, or taste them—we are inclined to discount them. But there is a reason these chemicals are given the designation "toxic," and it's not just because they make us sick at the time of exposure or because they can cause cancer years down the line. These chemicals can hurt us in ways that scientists are just beginning to understand. This chapter will explore in detail how these chemicals play out on our health.

The term "toxic" has become so common in our everyday conversation that we use it to describe everything from a noxious smell to a relationship gone sour. But what does it really mean in terms of environmental health? What are the actual origins, causes, and effects of toxicity? And where do the chemicals we use in our yards and households fit into the scheme of things? Scien-

tific research shows how these chemicals affect our bodies, but it isn't always easy to gain access to this research or understand the complex ways in which toxic chemicals behave when they come into contact with the body. Unfortunately, the passage of time is often what's needed to understand the long-term effects of a substance on the body; in other words, once the damage has been done—Love Canal, a case in point.

THE BIRTH OF "TOXIC"

Until the late 1970s, the word "toxic" barely made an appearance in the common American lexicon. But after the catastrophe at Love Canal in upstate New York, this changed.

At the turn of the last century, a neighborhood near Niagara Falls boasted a mile-long canal that was engineered under the direction of William T. Love, a developer who had planned a passage between the Niagara River and Lake Ontario. Love's vision was that his canal would provide the area's growing industries with hydroelectricity, but the project was never completed due to financial collapse and federal regulations. Eventually the City of Niagara Falls began using the canal as a municipal dump and Hooker Chemical Company was given permission to begin dumping chemical industrial waste there, soon purchasing it to use solely for this purpose. Hooker Chemical covered the canal with cement when it had finished using it and declared it safe.

When the City of Niagara Falls purchased land adjacent to the canal from Hooker Chemical in 1953, it was given a long list of warnings and signed a document releasing the company from liability associated with the land use. An elementary school and housing development were built on the property, attracting many young families. Heavy rains and snowstorms pushed a significant amount of the buried chemical waste to the surface, and by the late 1970s residents noticed an alarming incidence rate of illnesses in the community such as birth defects, cancers, neurological complaints, mental retardation, asthma, and miscarriages. According to the EPA's Superfund website, 56 percent of the children born in the area between 1974 and 1978 had birth defects.[41] [42]

Many of the chemicals we use in our yards and households (or their predecessors) were introduced into the home market in the 1950s—around the time the town of Niagara Falls thought it was okay to develop adjacent to the Hooker Chemical waste dump at Love Canal—and their toxic affect on the human body was indeed thought to be inconsequential in small amounts. Again, sadly, hindsight is our only avenue of understanding. We now have access to this scientific knowledge, but most of the important developments in understanding how toxic chemicals affect the body are very recent, many only dating back to 2009—such as the Scientific Statement published in 2009 by the Endocrine Society—the world's oldest organization of physicians and scientists who research and care for patients with hormonal problems. That said, many routine chemicals we use have endocrine-disrupting properties that are contributing to the development of myriad diseases.[43]

So how do we know if we are at risk?

TOXIC ACCUMULATION & INDIVIDUAL SUSCEPTIBILITY

When the body does not fully excrete dangerous chemicals, and they accumulate in the liver and fat stores of our bodies, we experience toxic accumulation, which exposes us to risk. Some of us are more at risk than others due to what is called "individual susceptibility"—a greater genetic predisposition to disease.[44] For example, a woman with a family history of breast cancer who is exposed to an estrogen-mimicking chemical in the environment might suffer devastating consequences, whereas another woman with no genetic predilection might not.

We are exposed to so many chemicals in our environment. Many of them persist and accumulate simply because they don't degrade, which means they will be here for generations to come, affecting our families. These pollutants diminish our air quality, litter our water supply, infiltrate our food chain, and, thus, wreak havoc on our bodies. Minimizing our exposure to toxic chemicals and pollutants is crucial to our health.

There is no doubt that using toxic products exposes you to increased risk each time you use them. And while it is a scientific fact that some people are more at risk or susceptible to some chemicals than others, few, if any, are immune.

ENVIRONMENTAL TOXINS

Many environmental toxins we are exposed to we have little control over. But there are plenty others that we do—those we use in our yards and homes. Minimizing our use of these toxic products will not only minimize the risk of exposure to us, our loved ones, and generations to come, but also our community at large. In this section we will look at the most common chemicals people use in their yards and homes. It's important to note that we are not only exposed to these chemicals when we use them and come into contact with their residues in our yards and homes, but also through our drinking water.[45] [46] [47]

Many of these chemicals have been on the market for many years, while others have been banned but are important case studies nevertheless. These chemicals are not only grouped here by what we use them for or how they work—pesticide, herbicide, fertilizer—but also by their chemical nature or basic chemical structure. Having a basic understanding of chemical structure is important because many of these toxic substances invade our bodies and mimic and/or disrupt important hormone and cell function, causing illness and disease.

Pesticides & Insecticides

Pesticides and insecticides, by their very design, are toxic. Pesticides are derived from chemicals used in World War II to combat malaria—specifically, DDT. Although DDT was banned for domestic use by the United States government in 1972, today's pesticides are nonetheless designed to be toxic to insects and rodents so that farmers can grow more crops per acre and preserve the crops en route to the market. The questions that the United States Department of Agriculture generally weighs involve precisely how toxic the pesticides are in relation to their benefits in bringing affordable, disease-free crops to market. But when initial public safety thresholds for pesticides were established, there was much less information about how low-level toxicity affects us. This is not surprising, and, in fact, President Clinton's Food Quality Protection Act of 1996 anticipated this and acknowledged that what is considered safe at one time will change with new information, requiring evaluation every ten years.[48]

The most common reasons people reach for pesticides in their gardens are to kill ants, snails, slugs, and unknown plant diseases. Most pesticides designed for home use do this by interfering with the neurologic system of the insect. Chemical pesticides are indiscriminate killers, often killing good insects (such as dragonflies

and butterflies) along with nuisance insects (such as mosquitoes). Many also harm bees; this is of particular concern since bees pollinate 40 percent of the food we eat.

In large doses, pesticides can cause neurologic poisoning in people, but this is usually only an issue in industrial accidents. In small doses, however, they can cause insidious but serious problems in people that may not be as obviously related to these chemicals. Research is teasing out these effects, and many chemicals we frequently use on our yards, or that are structurally similar to those chemicals, exhibit reproducible toxicities in the laboratory.

The most commonly used insecticides in homes and gardens in 2007 were:[49] [50]

- Carbaryl (a chemical in the carbamate class)
- Pyrethroids (botanical insecticides derived from chrysanthemums or similar synthetic compounds)
- Malathion (an organophosphate chemical)

ORGANOPHOSPHATE PESTICIDES

Organophosphate Pesticides all share a similar chemical structure. These pesticides are engineered to be neurotoxic, interfering with acetylcholinesterase, an enzyme involved in transmission of neurologic impulses in both insects and people. These pesticides lock on to the enzyme and don't let go. Normally, nerves are not touching each other. One nerve releases a substance called acetylcholine, which travels across the small space between the two nerves to the next nerve, carrying the neurologic impulse. Once it binds to receptors on the second nerve, the acetylcholine ignites the second nerve. Acetylcholinesterase normally degrades the acetylcholine at this point, preventing continued stimulation of the second nerve. But when pesticides block acetylcholinesterase, the second nerve is continually stimulated, which can lead to convulsions, paralysis, or muscles around the airway constricting enough to prevent breathing.

Pesticides marketed for residential use do not cause convulsions and asphyxia in people unless there is an accident and someone is exposed to a large amount; however, many organophosphates are now considered risks for more insidious problems: the potential both to cause cancer years down the line and to disrupt hormonal systems. Some common organophosphates have also been associated with ADHD, non-Hodgkin's lymphoma, abnormal nervous system development, testicular atrophy, and decreased sperm counts.[51] [52]

In 2007, 35 percent of the pesticide usage in the United States consisted of organophosphates, for a total of 3.3 million pounds.[53]

The most common organophosphate pesticides are:

- Malathion
- Chlorpyrifos (limited in sale for residential use since 2000 except in ant and roach baits, but still makes the EPA's most commonly used pesticide list for homes and gardens)
- Acephate
- Naled
- Diazinon (limited in sale for residential use since 2000)
- Dimethoate
- Phosmet

ORGANOCHLORIDE PESTICIDES

Organochlorides are similar in structure and function to organophosphates and work by blocking acetylcholinesterase. DDT is the best-known organochloride pesticide. It is no longer available, but because so much is known about it, it's a good example of how similar chemicals work. Organochloride pesticides are both potential carcinogens and endocrine disruptors.

CARBAMATE PESTICIDES

Carbamates, like organophosphates, interfere with

acetylcholinesterase, and thus with nerve transmission. Carbamates are also highly toxic to honeybees. Carbaryl, the most commonly used residential carbamate in the United States, is illegal in Denmark, Sweden, Germany, and the UK. Carbaryl is likely a carcinogen and can cause abnormal sperm and decreased sperm counts. Carbamates are both potential carcinogens and endocrine disruptors.[54]

The most commonly used carbamate is Carbaryl.

PYRETHRIN PESTICIDES

Pyrethrins occur naturally in the seed cases of chrysanthemums. In small amounts they repel insects, but in large amounts they are neurotoxins for insects and, in larger doses, for people, too. Natural pyrethins from chrysanthemums are relatively safe and degrade in a short period of time, but the many synthetic pyrethoids are associated with risks for endocrine disruption and abnormal neurodevelopment, likely because

DDT'S SILENT SPRING

DT was one of the first organochloride pesticides made. It was first used to control malaria in mosquito-infested areas during World War II; after the war, it was used as an agricultural pesticide. In 1962, Rachel Carson published Silent Spring, which documented the thinning of birds' eggshells from exposure to DDT. Carson's research suggested the possibility of increased cancer risk from exposure to DDT. In the wake of public outcry, DDT was banned in the US in 1972. Although DDT is now known to be a carcinogen and an endocrine disruptor, it is still used in some countries for insect control. DDT travels in air, water, and fish and is found in places as remote as the Himalayas. DDT is a neurodevelopment toxicant leading to abnormalities of the nervous system, as well as neurochemical changes. Studies link DDT to male infertility, diabetes, liver cancer, pancreatic cancer, and breast cancer.[57 58 59 60 61 62 63]

of chemical byproducts that arise during production and may be present in the finished product.[55] They are not known carcinogens.

The most commonly used pyrethoids are:[56]

- Allethrin
- Tralomethrin

Herbicides

Herbicides are used to control undesirable vegetation. For a farmer, this means weeds that will interfere with crops. For a backyard gardener, this might mean plants that are not where we want them—the ubiquitous herb purslane disrupting our patio, dandelions growing on our lawns, or milkweed (the only plant on which monarch butterflies can lay their eggs) in our flowerbeds. Undesirable vegetation in our yards can also mean invasive species such as Japanese barberry, which grows regardless of our efforts to pull it out.

Before we use an herbicide or weed killer to remedy this situation, however, we should better understand the toxicity of these products.

According to the EPA, the most commonly used residential herbicides are:[64][65]

- Glyphosate
- 2,4-D
- Diquat
- Dicamba
- Clopyralid
- Triclopyr
- 82,4-DP
- 2,4-DB
- MCPP and MCP are also widely used.

There are many different commercial mixtures of these compounds.

AMINO ACID DISRUPTERS

Glyphosate is the most widely used residential herbicide. It is designed to inhibit a plant's amino acid production when applied to its leaves. Disrupting protein production in a plant kills it. Similarly, people exposed to large amounts of amino acid disruptors suffer life-threatening consequences. Amino acids are the building blocks of proteins, and healthy proteins are crucial to healthy cells and healthy bodies. While the biggest component of our bodies by weight is water, the next largest is protein. 17 percent of our body weight is protein.

One of the most widely used herbicides in the world, glyphosate is considered relatively safe, partly because it breaks down quickly. But recent laboratory experiments have shown that its breakdown byproduct, AMPA, can disrupt human genes. While glyphosate is considered one of the safest pesticides, the EPA classifies it as a carcinogen, and studies show that it is also an endocrine disruptor.[66]

People exposed to large amounts of glyphosate can suffer health consequences such as cardiovascular collapse, difficulty breathing, kidney failure, shock, and nerve damage leading to brain abnormalities including difficulty thinking, Parkinson's disease, and coma.

SYNTHETIC PLANT HORMONES

Synthetic plant growth hormones, also called "auxin growth regulators," are fast-acting and cause uncontrolled growth, deformed new growth, and discoloration of the plants they are applied to. Bending and twisting of leaves and stems occurs immediately when these herbicides are used. Later the plants develop misshapen flowers, stems, and roots.[67]

The most commonly used synthetic plant hormones are:

- 2,4-D
- 2,4-DP
- 2,4-DB
- MCPP
- MCPA
- Dicamba
- Chlopyralid
- Triclopyr

CELL MEMBRANE DESTROYERS

These disrupt the outer layer of a plant's cells. Since cells are the building blocks of the plant, this leads to rapid plant death. Diquat is a bipyridylium herbicide that destroys cell membranes. Diquat is not a known carcinogen or endocrine disruptor.[68]

Fertilizers

Plants need oxygen, carbon, hydrogen, nitrogen, and phosphorus to grow. Oxygen, hydrogen, and carbon are readily available from air and water (the carbon comes from carbon dioxide in the air). On the other hand, while air contains 78 percent nitrogen, this nitrogen is not in a form that plants can use. Normally, soil bacteria "fix" the nitrogen, meaning they change it into ammonia, a form that plants can use. Some plants, such as clover and lupines, have nodules on their roots that harbor bacteria that fix nitrogen. Legumes like peas and beans also fix nitrogen, and some farmers use them to replenish soil near tomatoes or other plants that use lots of nutrients.

In the early 1900s, a process was developed in Germany that combined hydrogen and nitrogen in an industrial setting to make ammonia, the type of nitrogen that plants need. Ammonia is easily turned into nitric acid in a laboratory, and nitric acid makes effective explosives. So synthetic or laboratory-made fertilizer with ammonia helped farmers increase crop production for the war and also provided the main ingredient used to make explosives. After World War II, there were large leftover stores of fertilizer that were marketed to increase crop production and turn backyards lawns bright green.

Synthetic fertilizer marketed today contains nitrogen, phosphorus and potassium, which is noted as "NPK content" (K being the chemical initial for potassium). The excess nitrogen and phosphorus that plants do not use travels with rainwater into streams, ponds, and rivers. There, they cause an overgrowth of algae that saps the water of oxygen.

Excess nitrogen in the soil is converted to nitrates and nitrosamines by soil bacteria. These, in turn, travel with rainwater into our groundwater aquifer. Excess nitrates in drinking water given to babies or used to make formula ends up in babies' blood, where it binds the hemoglobin in their red blood cells, preventing the proper binding of oxygen. This leads to "blue baby syndrome," so called because the condition makes the baby look blue.[69]

Nitrates and nitrosamines have also been linked to cancers and endocrine disruption. In addition, some synthetic fertilizers have petroleum-based delivery systems and extenders; these petroleum-based molecules may disrupt the hormone system or increase the risks of some cancers.[70][71]

HEAVY METALS IN FERTILIZERS

While exposure to heavy metals does not usually occur from lawn chemicals, several fertilizers made from city sewage may contain heavy metals that pose risks to our health and water supply. Cadmium can come from industrial discharge into municipal sewage, and copper and lead can leach from residential pipes. Most treatment facilities do not remove all of these contaminants, so an emphasis is being placed on preventing them from entering the wastewater stream, especially from industrial sources.

Some heavy metals, including lead, naturally occur in soil in varying amounts. If these chemicals are present in the fertilizer we use, they will end up in our drinking water.

Heavy metals can pose huge health problems. Lead, for example, can cause neurotoxic-

ity—and the likelihood is even greater if exposure takes place in utero. Cadmium, meanwhile, is a known carcinogen.

Since there is a large amount of municipal sewage in the US, recycling it in a constructive way is a good thing if significant contaminants—yard and household chemicals—are not entering the sewage system. Headway is slowly being made in this direction.

Household Cleaning Products

Though lawn and garden chemicals are the focus of The Great Healthy Yard Project, household cleaning products deserve mention because they affect our health much the same way when we are exposed to them, and they enter our water supply when we pour them down the drain.

As we make our homes increasingly airtight to save energy on both heating and cooling, we eliminate fresh air circulation in the home. Many of the compounds we use in our homes contain volatile organic compounds, or VOCs. VOCs are carbon-based chemicals that evaporate at room temperature, so we breathe them in. They are in floor finishes, PVC pipes, and some "wrinkle-free" chemicals that release formaldehyde.

Our focus here, however, is on chemicals found in the home and business that are often disposed of down the drain and end up in the water supply, such as cleaning products, paint thinners, paints, and motor oil. These products often contain VOCs and other petroleum-based chemicals that are both endocrine disruptors and carcinogens. Many also contain phthalates, which are endocrine disruptors.

According to the EPA, indoor-air VOC concentrations are ten times that of those outdoor.[72] Many VOCs can cause irritation, allergies, and asthma, and chronic exposure poses a long-term risk for cancer.[73] In 2008, a study showed that a variety of household and industrial products, including paints, varnishes, floor polishes, and leather and upholstery cleaners can be ingested through the skin or by inhaling them (ethylene glycol alkyl ethers (EGAEs), 2-methoxyethanol, 2-ethoxyethanol, 2-isipopoxyethanol and 2-butoxyethanol). Once ingested, these chemicals are oxidized by the body into compounds that have toxic effects, including damage to the central nervous system and blood formation and reproductive abnormalities (aldehydes and alkoxyacetic acids).[74] Contaminating our water with these products by washing them down the drain puts our health, and the health of our communities, at risk.

Indoor dust picks up VOCs and other chemicals that are widely used in household products and, in turn—because dust clings to clothes, carpets, and hands—becomes a major source of exposure for children. A 2009 study showed that clothes dryer lint in the US and Germany was contaminated with polybrominated diphenyl ethers (PBDEs), which are proving

EARTHJUSTICE: CLEANING UP THE LAW

Earthjustice is an organization that advocates with remarkable success against powerful special interest groups at no cost to clients who have been injured by environmental insult. Keri Powell, an environmental lawyer for Earthjustice, has firsthand experience with chemical exposure: After law school, she worked for the New York Public Interest Research Group (NYPIRG) on an air pollution litigation project. The NYPIRG offices were in lower Manhattan, near the World Trade Center site. Returning to the site several weeks after the attacks on the Trade Center, Powell experienced headaches and slurring of speech, most likely due to the high benzene levels in the area.

Fearing continued exposure, Powell and her husband moved to Washington DC, where she began working for Earthjustice and became concerned about the toxic effects of household chemicals on people—particularly women, who do the majority of household work, and children, who are often exposed when their mothers work with volatile cleansers. Powell spoke to her mentor, Larry Shapiro, about the lack of consumer protection around household chemicals, and he urged her to open old statute books to see if there were any regulations that had been forgotten.

Powell took Shapiro's advice and found a New York State law written by then Governor Nelson A. Rockefeller and passed in 1971 that required the disclosure of all ingredients in household cleaners on labels. This law also gave the Department of Environmental Conservation (DEC) the ability to restrict any ingredients they felt were too risky. But what Powell found next stunned her: No companies had complied with this law, and there was no one enforcing compliance. In fact, the DEC, the agency responsible for enforcing the law, didn't even know about it.

Powell felt that enforcing this mandate was the most expeditious way to change both exposure and consumption. It would communicate risk to large numbers of people by disclosing ingredients on the packaging. Corporations are invariably unenthusiastic about such disclosures; after all, it took almost a decade to compel food manufacturers to report trans fat content on food labels—even though trans fats were known to be a risk factor for atherosclerotic heart disease, the single leading cause of death in America.

On February 17, 2009, Powell filed a brief arguing for demonstration of the safety of chemicals prior to marketing and for full disclosure on the contents of household chemicals. Powell first sent letters to the manufacturers of these products requesting full disclosure under the 1971 law, and received responses from only a few companies. She filed suits against companies that did not respond, including Proctor & Gamble, Colgate Palmolive, Church & Dwight and Reckitt Benckiser. In March of 2009, SC Johnson responded to the pressure and announced full disclosure of all chemical ingredients in its products on labels and on its website.[78]

Powell's court fight is important on many levels. While this law is unique to New York, thanks to the foresight of Governor Rockefeller, once ingredients are disclosed in New York, they will be available to the general public. Hopefully this will set a nationwide precedent requiring disclosure on labeling.

to be persistent, organic pollutants that find their way onto clothes during routine usage (they are widely used as additives in flame retardants, stain repellants, and electronic equipment).[75] They are found in the environment, human blood, breast milk, and body tissues. Their structure and toxicity is similar to PCBs. Like PCBs, they are potential carcinogens and endocrine disruptors. Many cleaning products that contain VOCs can easily be replaced with old-fashioned home remedies that are remarkably effective. At the very least, we can use these cleaners infrequently, and only as a last resort.

Chlorine bleach in cleaning products also presents a problem when it enters the water cycle. It combines with naturally occurring organic products, such as plant debris in natural waterways, forming chlorinated organic compounds that, like organochloride pesticides, can both cause cancer and disrupt the endocrine system. Scents used in many cleaning products also have endocrine disrupting chemicals that we both inhale and that end up in wastewater.

Many household cleaning products consist of a few relatively safe and effective ingredients combined with many noxious ingredients to impart color and smell.[76] These ingredients are also preservatives that give the cleaner a very long shelf life. These products also often contain agents that keep the active ingredient dissolved so we don't have to shake them before use.

We have come to equate the scent of these volatile organic compounds with the scent of cleanliness. It's important to begin to associate these scents, and colors, with branding and marketing rather than cleanliness. These are not clean scents; they are chemical scents. Clean is the absence of infringing scents on the surrounding environment. Clean means we can smell fresh air, real flowers and plants, or what is cooking in the kitchen.

Paints, paint thinners, and motor oil should

be disposed of on household material recovery days or at disposal sites, not down the drain.[77]

Pharmaceuticals

Pharmaceuticals are not completely removed from water by any form of wastewater treatment. They are found in small amounts in the water supplies of every major city, and they get there in the wastewater stream because of the confluence of drinking water and wastewater. Pharmaceuticals that are excreted in urine or washed off of our skin will inevitably end up in our wastewater, but excess medication needs to be responsibly disposed of. Pharmaceuticals that are designed to have a myriad of positive effects on our bodies have a diverse array of adverse effects when we don't need them, which is why it's so important to keep them out of the water supply. Birth control pills, chemotherapy agents, and antidepressants are among the most commonly found medications in drinking water.[79] [80] [81] [82] [83] [84] [85]

CARCINOGENS & ENDOCRINE DISRUPTORS

The effects of overexposure to chemicals is often obvious: people experience seizures, trouble breathing, and shock, among other symptoms. However, even if we're unaware of any immediate risk, there are two major ways that exposure to small amounts of offending chemicals can have long-term detrimental effects: carcinogenesis and endocrine disruption.

"Carcinogenesis" means "the production of cancer"—and we have known for a long time that chemicals that don't appear to harm us can lead to cancer many years down the line. More recently, however, scientists have been researching "endocrine disruptors." Endocrine disruptors can also cause long-term harm, particularly to children and unborn babies.

Understanding both of these mechanisms in broad terms is important since lawn and garden chemicals, household cleaning supplies, and pharmaceuticals act as both endocrine disruptors and cancer-causing agents when we are exposed to them. Since the amount of exposure involved is so small, a direct line between the exposure and consequence is difficult to discern in people. But concerns raised by scientists have led to both epidemiologic studies of populations that confirm these relationships and laboratory experiments that reproduce them.

Some cancers are caused by chemicals directly damaging the genetic material of cells, and here the risk is greater at higher doses of exposure. However, hormone disruption can cause many problems, including cancer, even in much, much smaller doses than were previously thought to be harmful.

Carcinogens: DNA Destroyers

Carcinogens are chemicals that can cause cancer by disrupting the genetic composition of the body's cells—their deoxyribonucleic acid (DNA).

DNA is the genetic blueprint for the development and functioning of all known living organisms. Think of DNA as a cell "cookbook." The cookbook gives each cell direction on how to reproduce, offering specific recipes and instructions for making specific proteins. DNA's protein cookbook is exhaustive. Some of these proteins are the very building blocks of cells, while others comprise hormones. Some, called "suppressor proteins," prevent damaged DNA from dividing. "Pointer proteins," meanwhile, adhere to damaged blood vessels and act as beacons so that repair cells can locate injuries and repair them. And this is just a small sampling of the vast array of remarkable proteins that DNA produces.

When DNA is damaged, however, it encodes proteins in unpredictable, flawed ways, causing the cells themselves to function abnormally. When those cells replicate, they pass down these abnormalities to their daughter cells, and those cells pass it on to their daughter cells. The effect of replicating flawed DNA is that all cells in this "cell line," behave abnormally. Repeated abnormal cellular behavior is what we call cancer.

Abnormal DNA is "made" in several ways. Sometimes it is hereditary. Take the example of the BRCA gene. BRCA genes, which are passed down from mother to daughter, normally produce tumor-suppressing proteins. As one might expect, an abnormal BRCA gene produces flawed tumor suppressing proteins; hence, an increased incidence of breast and ovarian tumors.[86] (Fortunately, there are BRCA gene tests available.)

Abnormal DNA can also be the result of random genetic mutations—inexplicable glitches during cell replication resulting in a bad copy. Toxic chemicals, heavy metals, and radiation can cause such glitches. These substances can be so potent that they interfere with the intertwining of DNA's double helix. The result is the same. Carcinogenesis can cause cells to divide abnormally, resulting in cancer.

Organochlorides, organophosphates, and carbamate pesticides are all carcinogens. The weed killer glyphosate is also a carcinogen.[87]

Endocrine Disruptors

Any discussion of endocrine disruptors needs to start with a primer on hormones. Mention "hormones" and the mind instantly leaps to the reputation of male testosterone or the female sex hormones involved in menstruation and pregnancy. However, human hormones are multitudinous and play a much bigger role than most of us know.

Hormones are responsible for regulating such vital activities in the human body as growth, reproduction, and homeostasis. They are responsible for regulating metabolism; glucose and fat absorption; activating or suppressing the immune system; inducing or inhibiting apoptosis (programmed cell death); developing male and female sex and brain differences; survival instincts; regulation of the kidneys; emotions; and much more.

Hormones are produced by the endocrine system, which consists of three parts: the section of the brain called the hypothalamus, the multiple glands that secrete hormones, and the hormones themselves. Located at the base of the brain, the hypothalamus is attached to, and responsible for, regulating the pituitary gland—known as the "master gland" because it is involved in the regulation of many of the other endocrine glands.

When endocrine glands secrete hormones into the bloodstream, the hormones circulate throughout the body. Arriving at their target organs, hormones bind to specific organ receptors. Like keyholes, these receptors are shaped so that only the specific hormones that regulate them can fit into their particular binding sites. When they bind, the hormones change the shapes of the receptors, triggering either the release of another hormone or a change in action of the target cells.

Endocrine disruptors can disrupt all of the systems regulated by hormones, and they can also cause cancer. The problem begins when hormone mimics or blockers bind with abnormal cells. Endocrine disruptors can cause cancer by binding with abnormal cells that would have otherwise been suppressed by our immune system (breast and prostate among them), ultimately stimulating the production of so many abnormal cells that the immune system is overwhelmed. Cancer isn't the only problem, however.

Unlike the effects of carcinogens, the effects of endocrine disruptors are not proportional to the dose of exposure. With carcinogens, in general, a person needs to be bombarded before the problems appear. With endocrine disruptors, a little goes a very, very long way. Life-altering consequences may occur from minute exposure, especially when a person is particularly susceptible. Children and fetuses—with their new, developing systems—are particularly vulnerable. Some hormone disruptors may not affect a mother visibly at all, but they will persist in her body and affect the development of the fetus when she gets pregnant. When a fetus is exposed to endocrine disruptors, a multitude of abnormalities can develop.

Hormones are responsible for the development of many body systems of the fetus—brain, sexual, and metabolic development, among others. If the mother's hormonal system is thrown off by endocrine disrupting chemicals, the developing fetus reacts as though there is too much or too little hormone present, and development goes awry. How development is derailed or the adult body is affected depends on which hormone is disrupted from doing its normal job.

HORMONE MIMICS

Endocrine disruptors are chemicals that disrupt the normal function of our actual hormones in two basic ways. Some endocrine disruptors, called "hormone mimics," act like skeleton keys: they can bind to the natural hormone's target organ receptor, because a portion of each one is shaped similarly enough to the real hormone for the receptor to be fooled—and once they bind, they can turn the key and open the lock, activating the receptor. These mimics are called "agonists" because they act like excess hormones. The problem here is that the stimulation persists, when it should be fleeting. There is also a subgroup of these hormone mimics that so overwhelm a receptor that, ultimately, the receptor no longer responds. A mimic enters the lock, turns the key, and causes a release of hormones, but then it sticks inside, making it impossible for any other key to enter and turn it.

HORMONE BLOCKERS

The other group of hormone disruptors is the "hormone blocker." This group is also shaped like a key and binds the receptors. However, in this group's case, it never stimulates the receptor; it just stays stuck, not activating hormone release—like a bad key stuck in a lock. These disruptors are

THE PERSISTENT LEGACY OF PCBs

Agricultural corporation Monsanto started producing PCBs in 1930. PCBs are organo-chloride chemicals, as are DDT and numerous other pesticides. Effective as insulators and fire retardants, PCBs were used in transformers and capacitors to coat electrical wiring, engine oils, and building materials including floor finishes, caulking, and paint. From 1929 to 1977, General Electric (GE) had two plants that manufactured capacitors on the Hudson River in New York, one at Hudson Falls and one at Fort Edward. Together, they discharged 1.3 million pounds of PCBs into the Hudson before their manufacture was banned.[88] Swallows in the area had high enough levels of PCBs in their bodies and eggs to qualify the birds themselves as hazardous waste.

When PCBs were found downstream in spite of attempts to bury them, people realized containment was not possible. In 1984, the area became a Superfund site—a site designated by the EPA as unsuitable for use due to toxic waste—because of the contamination of the fish there and the increased risk of cancer, immune disease, thyroid abnormalities, and reproductive abnormalities the area presented. Once it designates an area as a Superfund site, the EPA works with the offending companies to decrease the toxic pollution in the most efficient and responsible way, eventually remediating the site for safe use. Dredging for PCBs by GE is ongoing in 2013, and recreation on the Hudson is still curtailed.[89]

Likewise, when PCBs were found in the sediment of the lakebed and in fish on the west shore of Lake Michigan, it was discovered that the Outboard Marine Corp of Waukegan, Illinois had dumped PCBs into the Waukegan River, which drains into the lake. The community suffered fish kills, health issues, and economic devastation. In 1990, it also became a Superfund site. PCBs are carcinogenic as well as endocrine disruptors—specifically, estrogen mimics.[90]

called "blockers" or "antagonists" because they prevent real hormones from functioning.

GENDER BENDERS

Endocrine disruptors that mimic estrogen are often called "gender benders" because they can have a feminizing effect on males and affect the onset of puberty and ovulation in females. Hormones are what "shape" our brains, both during brain development and during puberty. The area of the brain that changes during early development in response to sex hormones is called the anteroventral periventricular nucleus (AVPV). Located in the hypothalamus, AVPV contains "sexually dimorphic cells," or cells that are responsible for sex differences in the brain. Endocrine disruptors that mimic estrogen can interfere with the development of AVPV and lead to feminization of male brains.[91] [92] When the neurons in the hypothalamus of the female brain are disrupted, it can bring about the early onset of

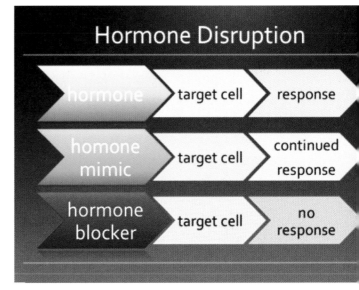

puberty and ovulation. Exposure to endocrine disruptors can also result in diminished sperm counts in infants and men and diminished Y chromosome production (a lower male to female birthrate).[93] [94] [95]

THYROID DISORDER AND CHILD BRAIN DEVELOPMENT

The thyroid gland is shaped like a tiny, two-inch-long bow tie and sits in the neck, just in front of the larynx. Thyroid hormone affects nervous system function, heart and cardiovascular systems, muscle strength, menstrual cycles, the metabolic system, and weight. If a person's thyroid is not producing enough thyroid hormone, they often experience fatigue and weight gain. In serious cases of low thyroid, patients can develop myxedema coma. This means they cannot maintain their metabolic function and their temperature drops below normal. Their heart rate and breathing drop and the brain cannot function.

Hypothyroidism in pregnant women has long been associated with mental retardation in the developing fetus. Recently, however, scientists have begun to unravel the many ways in which thyroid hormone affects fetal brain development, finding that minute abnormalities in thyroid hormone in the mother can lead to a spectrum of neurological abnormalities in the developing fetus.[96] [97] [98]

Endocrine disruptors can be responsible for corrupting pregnant women's thyroid hormones, and by disrupting thyroid hormone physiology they disrupt brain and central nervous system development for children exposed in utero.[99] This is now thought to be one of the causes for autism and ADHD. PCBs are chemicals that have been around a long time and are organochlorides, similar in structure to many pesticides. They are known to disrupt thyroid hormone and lead to increased incidences of neurologic problems in areas where pregnant women have experienced significant exposure to PCBs, and also in laboratory animals that have been intentionally exposed.[100] [101]

AUTISM AND ADHD

Theo Colborn, one of the first to publish data on endocrine-disrupting chemicals, and one of the environmental scientists who helped coin the term, published a literature review in 2004 in Environmental Health Perspectives noting that autism is the fastest-growing developmental disability, increasing at a rate of 10 to 17 percent annually. She showed that a lesion thought to be responsible for autism develops just before or shortly after neural tube closure in the fetus, around the sixth or seventh week of gestation in humans. Colborn tracked the historical correlation between the increase in exposure to endocrine-disrupting hormones and the population's increase in autism and ADHD. Observing that the first generation exposed to high levels of chemical toxins in the womb was the generation born in the 1950s, Colborn noted that this group was having children precisely when there appeared to be an increase in neurodevelopment disorders (in the 1970s).[102] [103] [104] [105] [106]

DIABETES AND OBESITY

Hormones regulate our use and storage of energy in the body. Hormone-disrupting chemicals can disrupt the normal communication involved in these functions. The twin epidemics of diabetes and obesity currently in our society may be only partly a function of bad dietary choices. These may also be the result of toxins in our environment. The hormone insulin, secreted by the pancreas, is responsible for regulating glucose uptake by cells; the hormones leptin and estrone are secreted by fat. Leptin normally leads to a decrease in appetite and an increase in metabolism. If hormone-disrupting chemicals interfere with these hormones, they can contribute to obesity and diabetes.

The links between hormone-disrupting chemicals and diabetes are described in an article in 2009 showing that the prevalence of diabetes correlated with the body burden of PCBs and that perinatal exposure to low doses of BPA affects body weight. A 2008 study also demonstrated an association between diabetes and pesticide exposure among licensed pesticide applicators.[107] [108] [109] [110]

BREAST AND REPRODUCTIVE CANCERS

Exposure to endocrine-disrupting chemicals, including those in common lawn chemicals, is thought to be a risk for breast cancer, since disruptors bind to abnormal cells that have estrogen receptors and encourage their growth. Many women were given estrogen to relieve symptoms experienced with the natural diminution of estrogen when they were menopausal or perimenopausal. This worked well until it was discovered estrogen therapy increased incidence of breast cancer.

The danger to a woman's reproductive system when she is given estrogen has a difficult history. The most well-known example is the story of diethylstilbestrol, or DES, one of the first synthetic estrogens. Manufactured in the US from 1938 until 1971, DES was prescribed to pregnant women to prevent miscarriage.[111] At the time it was thought that increasing the levels of a pregnant woman's estrogen would prevent her from miscarrying.

In 1971, a study showed an increased incidence of clear cell adeno cancer (CCA) of the vagina in girls as young as eight years old who had been exposed to DES in the womb.[112]

Vaginal CCA is a rare form of cancer; discovering it in young girls was so unusual that physicians began looking for a common thread between the cases. Shortly after the study results were released, the FDA issued a bulletin advising physicians to stop prescribing DES to pregnant women. Physicians were told to look back in their records and notify women who had taken the drug. Ongoing studies were begun on women given DES during pregnancy, and on their daughters and sons.

The women given DES during pregnancy appeared to have a slightly higher risk of breast cancer.[113] Their sons had an increase in noncancerous, epididymal cysts. But their daughters have suffered the most. Not only do they have an increased incidence of CCA, they are also at a high risk for having abnormal reproductive tracts. A healthy uterus looks like a pear with the round side up. Many of the "DES daughters" have T-shaped uteruses or atretic uteruses—uteruses that are a remnant of the reproductive tract and may have no cavity at all. This has led to an increased incidence of ectopic pregnancies—pregnancies where the fetus is implanted in a place other than the uterus—which cause pain and bleeding and can be life-threatening.

DES daughters also suffer from premature deliveries, miscarriages, and infertility. Now that some of these women are getting older, doctors are discovering that DES daughters over forty are two-and-a-half times more likely than the general population to develop breast cancer. As these women's daughters are now having children, there is an ongoing study of the third DES generation.[114]

DES is no longer an active threat. Once new scientific information demonstrated its irrefutable harm, the federal government acted swiftly and decisively to ban its use. According to the Center for Disease Control (CDC), five to ten million pregnant women and their children were exposed to DES.

MINIMIZING RISK THROUGH INCREASED AWARENESS

Public awareness about environmental toxins continues to grow in the wake of disasters like Love Canal. Incidents involving toxic exposure, which are host to all manner of injuries, illnesses, and birth defects, have become everyday concerns. There are more documentary exposés than ever, and many of us have seen blockbuster hits such as Silkwood and Erin Brockovich.

With increased awareness, usage of pesticides has decreased 57 percent from all pesticides used in 1980. In fact, total pesticide usage also decreased between 1980 and 2007, dropping from 228 million pounds to 98 million pounds per year in the United States. But much of this is due to changes in agricultural practices. Household use is unabated.[115] The incidence of ADHD, autism, diabetes, and breast cancer has increased in parallel with the increased usage of synthetic pesticides, weed killers, and fertilizers in the home.

As we have seen, these chemicals (or similar ones) cause abnormal neurologic development, abnormal metabolic function, and cancer. Using synthetic pesticides, weed killers, and fertilizers in our yards and gardens guarantees risk and exposure to these chemicals, not only through our drinking water but also through tracking them into our homes, absorbing them through our skin, and inhaling them.

The truth is, we can't know how or if we'll suffer illness as a result of this exposure, since illness is never a simple equation. But we can assume that some of us will suffer, and we know that those at greatest risk are our children and those with genetic predispositions.

With over 80,000 chemicals in widespread use, changing our behavior—replacing toxic lawn and household products with healthy alternatives—is the fastest way to minimize the risk to us, our loved ones, and our communities.

CHAPTER 4:

Creating a Restorative Yard—Take the Pledge!

"A place belongs forever to whoever claims it hardest, remembers it most obsessively, wrenches it from itself, shapes it, renders it, loves it so radically that he remakes it in his own image."
—Joan Didion

"The house is a castle which the King cannot enter," Ralph Waldo Emerson wrote, characterizing a deeply held belief that our property belongs to us alone. Yet, as we have seen, there are some things that infiltrate and threaten our castle that are not under our individual control.

Our drinking water is, in many ways, the life-blood of our homes, yet to keep our water pure we are not only dependent on our choices, but also our neighbors'. The choices we and our neighbors make combine to have a big effect on our local community, and contribute in smaller ways to the global community. We share our toxic footprint with the world, but we can also share solutions. Together, our yards contain most of the land in the United States, so great improvement can be achieved in our water quality by working together to make simple changes commonplace. We can amend our toxic practices and minimize our impact by simply choosing not to use toxic pesticides, weed killers, and fertilizers in our yards or dispose of cleaning supplies and pharmaceuticals down our drains. We can also educate our neighbors so they understand that water is one of our most important shared resources and that community participation is essential to the protection of water quality.

There are a few obstacles we face in embracing Minimal Impact Management practices in and around our homes, but they are easily surmountable. There is widespread lack of understanding of just how important making these changes are to our water quality and to our families' health. In addition, we have a feeling that what we do as individuals is inconsequential and that it will take extra time and money to make real change—and corporate marketing reinforces these misconceptions. However, we will not have clean drinking water until we stop using synthetic chemicals in our homes and gardens.

This chapter will explore the ways in which we can reform our toxic habits by replacing them with easy alternatives at no additional investment of our time and money. The only obstacle left to stare down is our susceptibility to the big-company marketing that promotes friendly, green-grass competition with our neighbor. The reality is, an emerald green lawn, off-season, is a sure sign that someone is contributing to the contamination of the water supply and putting our families at risk. Certainly the research findings on the toxic effects of even small amounts of synthetic chemicals on our health, and the fact that they are found in most of our drinking water, is incentive enough to get us over any hurdles to practicing Minimal Impact Management in and around our homes. Our health, and that of our families, depends on this certainty.

NATURAL LAWN & GARDEN CARE IS SIMPLE

As we learned in earlier chapters, lawns do not absorb and filter water nearly as well as trees and shrubs. Rainwater and water from our garden hoses passes through our yards, becoming both ground and surface water and eventually our drinking water supply. If you use fertilizers and pesticides on your lawn or in your garden, they wash with the rainwater into the water supply.

There is no question of whether you are contributing to the contamination of the water supply; you are.

So what are your choices?

Contrary to what you may think, caring for your lawn and garden without the use of deadly chemicals is easy and does not require expert advice. Below are a few tips to help you care for your lawn and yard with minimal impact.

Soil Protection

Much of caring for a lawn naturally is the mechanical care necessary to improve soil quality and plant health. Helpful bacteria grow in the top layer of soil. Minimizing the use of blowers prevents erosion and also allows these microbes to flourish. Deep rototilling of the soil, on the other hand, predisposes it to erosion and destroys roots and helpful microbes, so this is not something you want to do on a regular basis.

Aerating regularly, in the fall or spring, is one of the best things you can do for your lawn. Aerating relieves the compaction that occurs from compression by people, animals, and vehicles, including lawn mowers. Compaction is also caused by erosion and dry weather, particularly in soils that are predisposed to it. Plants and beneficial soil bacteria need air to thrive.

For a small yard, a spading fork will work to remove compaction and allow air to penetrate

the soil. For larger areas, you may want to rent an aerator or hire someone to aerate for you. A power aerator removes small cores of soil, loosening the earth and allowing air to reach more of the soil. Aerating regularly is particularly important in areas with high traffic. If your soil is compacted and you aerate it, you will be surprised at how much easier it is to keep your yard looking good.

Wise Weeding

Eliminate weeds with boiling water (not near stone, which may crack), hand weeding, vinegar, or clove oil; these work well on lawns and patios (just pour liberally over the top), but hand weeding is best near flowers and shrubs. Before your weed problem gets out of hand, outcompete weeds by overseeding with a small amount of grass seed (much smaller than is needed to start a lawn). Repair bare spots in early spring and again in late summer or early fall. Remember, having a few weeds is okay. Advertising tells us diversity on our lawn or in our garden is undesirable, but this is unrealistic and untrue. Many common weeds are not only edible, but also beneficial to your health. The dandelion is a perfect example.

Mow Right

The length of the roots will mirror the shoots, so letting your grass grow to four inches long before you mow it will ensure long roots. Deeper roots allow the grass to gain more nutrients and to get water more easily during a dry spell. Mow your lawn when the grass reaches four to five inches and cut it down to a three-inch height. Never remove more than one third of the grass blade. Don't leave the grass at more than four inches for the winter. Also, after cutting your grass, leave the clippings. Clippings replete the nitrogen, cool the soil, and retain water. Leaving the clippings will not cause "thatch." A healthy lawn has an abundance of microorganisms that break down thatch. Thatch usually occurs on heavily fertilized turf that is compacted, acidic, poorly drained, and can't breathe. If your lawn has thatch, try core aeration to relieve it. Last, keep your mower blades sharp so they cut and don't tear. Tearing depletes water and leaves grass vulnerable to disease.[116]

Biological Pesticides

Biologically based pesticides and herbicides are becoming more popular due to increased awareness of the ill effects of regular pesticide use. Biologically based pesticides are thought to be a safer alternative. Biological pesticides include pheromones that attract and trap insects. Milky spore, a fungus that is harmless to people but attacks Japanese beetle larvae, is an example of a biological pesticide. Corn gluten is sometimes used as a natural pre-emergent weed killer, as it inhibits seeds from growing but does not affect existing plants. Corn gluten will inhibit both grass seed and weed seed, however, so it is only useful on an established lawn that you are not overseeding. Applied in April or mid-August, corn gluten inhibits annual weed seeds, including crab grass and stilt grass. Beneficial predators such as ladybugs and tiny wasps are also examples of biological pesticides.

Grassing Up

How do you choose the right grass? Choose a grass mixture that grows well in your region throughout the seasons. Speak with your local university cooperative extension, garden club, or other local resource to help you make the decision. For example, The Lady Bird Johnson Wildflower and Native Plant Center, located at the University of Texas in Austin, has developed HABITURF, a patented turf grass mixture native to Texas that is drought resistant, requires less weeding and mowing, and stands up to foot traffic as well. HABITURF is beautiful, feels good underfoot, and thrives without pesticides or fertilizer.

You can also speak with your university cooperative extension to see if there are grasses best adapted to your yard. Many big box stores sell grass seeds that are selected because the grass they produce generate large quantities of seed rather than using its energy to fortify its roots and produce more grass blades. For farms that produce grass seed, the prolific generation of seed per acre translates to a crop that can be sold cheaply. The Internet is a great resource for information and sources of seeds. If you have a problem with stilt grass, an invasive Japanese herb that is ubiquitous in Bedford, consider aerating and overseeding with a late perennial rye to outcompete the stilt grass. Mowing it before it goes to seed is also important.

Water Log

If you've chosen the correct type of grass, you should only have to water a few weeks in the summer, about an inch a week in the early morning. The right grass will go dormant when the conditions are not favorable (too cold or dry). When the grass goes dormant, it fades so it is no longer vibrant green in color, and it stops growing. It is still alive, however, and when conditions improve it will once again turn deep green and start growing both above and below ground. Do water germinating seeds until they emerge. Do not overwater and allow puddling.

Fertile Ground

Test your soil. If there is a nutrient deficit, the nutrients in the soil may need to be replaced. A simple soil test for nitrogen and phosphorus will tell you if your soil is lacking in these nutrients, and your local cooperative extension or garden center can help you calculate how much supplement you need to replace these nutrients. If your lawn is lacking a nutrient, you can replace it with an organic fertilizer rather than one made from petroleum. Organic fertilizers need to be put down when soil microbes are active—when it's 65 degrees or warmer. Be sure to fertilize in the fall, not the spring, because fall is when root growth is the greatest. Don't over-fertilize; this will put stress on your plants. Consider topdressing with compost or compost tea. Check the pH of your soil and adjust it with organic amendments, like lime, if necessary. Soil testing kits are available at many garden centers. University co-ops often do soil testing as well; their tests are more comprehensive, and they can offer advice.

Vegetable Gardens

Backyard vegetable gardens are beautiful, provide nutrition for our families, and attract and nourish birds and other pollinators. Gardens illustrate that what we put in our yards ends up in our bodies, in this case very directly. When we eat vegetables from our garden, our bodies

absorb their nutrients. If we use synthetic chemicals in our gardens, which planted vegetables absorb, these chemicals not only end up in our water but also directly in our body. We can protect our families from absorbing pesticides if we don't apply them to food we are growing. Likewise, if we don't apply these chemicals to our yards, they will not end up in our drinking water.

A vegetable garden is also a wonderful way to learn natural gardening and soil culture—anything that doesn't turn out well can be replaced next year. Try experimenting with a small garden and expanding it as you get more involved, or even just planting a few containers of tomatoes and herbs to get started. If you have room, consider a few chickens to eat bugs in your vegetable garden and on your lawn. Chickens provide both natural pest control and fertilizer. If your chickens are eating the bugs on your lawn, you won't need pesticides.

DANDELIONS ARE DANDY

*I*talian painter and award-winning chef and cookbook author Ed Giobbi is a dandelion fan—a fan of that much-maligned "weed" we now know to be both edible and nutritious. Giobbi thinks dandelions are beautiful and fun for children when they go to seed, but his favorite attribute of dandelions is their culinary versatility.

One of his favorite recipe creations is a vegetable dish he calls "Verdura Trovata," or found vegetables. He was served Verdura Trovata for the first time at his aunt Zia Pippina's farm in the town of Le Marche, in central Italy. Giobbi would accompany her into the fields in the springtime, after all of the root vegetables were harvested and before the spring planting had begun, and they would harvest wild greens such as the dandelion. Giobbi says dandelion greens are most palatable in the spring, and that wild dandelion greens are tastier than those grown in a garden with purchased seeds.[117]

VERDURA TROVATA

By Edward Giobbi

Chop collected wild greens, including dandelions, purslane, lambsquarters, and redroot. Add kale, Swiss chard, and cabbage leaves, also chopped. Also add diced potatoes, about one large potato for every 1½ pounds of greens. Boil the greens and potatoes in salted water, drain and reserve ½ cup of the liquid. Sauté two cloves of garlic and an onion for every 1½ pounds of greens. As the garlic browns, add the greens. Add reserved liquid as needed and cook until tender. If desired, add a small piece of chopped hot pepper.

WILD DANDELION GREENS WITH BEANS

By Edward Giobbi

½ cup of Great Northern Italian white beans, dried and soaked overnight (red beans can be substituted)

Cook dried beans ½ hour before adding dandelion greens (if canned beans are substituted, skip this step)

1 tbsp olive oil

1 small onion, chopped

2 garlic cloves, minced

4 cups of wild dandelion greens, washed and blanched for 1 to 2 mins in salted water

Drain the greens. Sauté garlic and onion, beans. Add drained greens and top with extra virgin olive oil and grated Parmesan cheese

DANDELION FRITTATA
By Edward Giobbi

Collect dandelion greens and wash thoroughly. Chop. Boil in water or stock for 5 to 10 minutes, depending on size and age of greens. Scramble several eggs; add milk, salt, and pepper. Mix with greens and make a soft frittata. If desired, add a little Parmesan cheese prior to cooking

....

MIXED SPRING SALAD WITH DANDELION GREENS
By Edward Giobbi

Combine mixed spring salad greens and tender young dandelion greens. Sauté anchovies and minced garlic in extra virgin olive oil and use to dress greens. Top with shaved Parmesan cheese.

Giobbi's recipes are not only delicious, they're healthy. Dandelion greens have more Vitamin A than spinach and more Vitamin C than tomatoes. Dandelions have been used in traditional Chinese medicine for over 1,000 years. And health food stores carry tinctures and teas for its many medicinal uses. Growing your own dandelion greens will save you money as well, since they sell for about $32 per pound, more than most other vegetables—another example of their true value.

If you have an infestation in your garden, there are three basic certified organic remedies that deal with most problems and are safe enough to use if you have to. One is a certified organic insecticidal soap. This works only when directly applied to soft-bodied insects like aphids and spider mites, making their cells leaky. Another is Spinosad. Spinosad is a metabolite produced by the fermentation of the bacteria S. spinosa. It controls caterpillars, cabbage worms, leafminers, slugs, and hornworms. It also hurts bees, so it should only be used in the early morning or evening, once bees have gone to their hives. And last is Neem oil. Neem oil is made from the seeds of the evergreen neem tree and is both a repellent and a hormonal disruptor for insects. It has been used for centuries in India in soaps.

Composting

Feeding your garden with compost not only avoids chemicals, it also cuts down on waste.

Composting yard material, including mulched leaves, plant material, vegetable scraps, and eggshells, is really easy. How does a compost pile work? Through microbial metabolism. The elevated temperature at the center of a compost pile is the result of microbial metabolism as plant matter is digested. For this reason, it is important to build your compost pile to about three feet high and three feet in diameter if possible.

Layering soil with compost material helps, as does turning it so that all of the compost will have a turn being in the center, where it is the warmest and where the most degradation occurs. Mulching leaves before they are put on the pile will allow them to degrade more rapidly. If you are willing to tend a compost pile for a year, you will have dark, rich compost to add to your garden. Finely mulched leaves can also be used directly on garden beds to enrich soil and prevent weeds from growing.

Composting decomposing food scraps inside requires a little more attention to prevent the pile from getting smelly or bug-infested. Getting started on an outdoor compost pile, however, is easy, and you will develop your own technique over time. Try putting the pile in a convenient spot, but not in a wetland buffer. Include leaf matter, vegetable scraps, and egg shells. Chicken, horse, or cow manure is a wonderful addition. Do not add diseased plants to your compost, and do not add plants that have been sprayed with pesticide for a local infestation. Weeds can be added to a compost pile, but the weed seeds need to be killed by the elevated temperature that is reached in the center of the pile. Your local garden club is a wonderful resource for more information on composting.

ADD TO COMPOST

- Plants
- Vegetable scraps
- Leaves
- Eggshells
- Manure: horse, chicken, cow, sheep, or goat

DON'T ADD TO COMPOST

- Oils or oil-containing foods (like salad with dressing)
- Meat
- Fish
- Dog or cat waste

- Cheese
- Bones
- Egg whites or yolks
- Diseased plants
- Plants sprayed with pesticides

PAYING ENVIRONMENTAL PROTECTION FORWARD

Now that you have provided a beautiful, healthy, safe lawn for your family to enjoy, you may wonder if there is more you can do in your yard to help improve water quality.

The answer is a resounding yes!

Many of us have areas in our yards that go unused and can easily be developed to aid in water protection. And as we'll see in the suggestions below, water protection takes many forms. Choosing to employ some of these environmental protective measures will not only do much to protect your local water quality, and thus your family's and community's health, but also wildlife habitat crucial to a healthy water cycle. In addition, it's an opportunity for creative fun outdoors.

Go Native!

Finding an exotic, non-native plant that is new to us is exciting, particularly if we are captivated by its beauty. When we bring it home and it flourishes, there's nothing better, right?

Wrong.

Alien plants often remain untouched by our native insects and predators, and some crowd out our native plants. Invasive plants in New York State, combined with deer browsing, are responsible for the very slow forest regeneration in the southern half of the state.[118] This is because many of the invasive plants "leaf out" several weeks before the native plants, robbing native saplings of nutrition and light. Japanese barberry is among those invasive plants that are allelopathic, meaning they release a chemical that inhibits native plants from growing. Vines such as Oriental bittersweet strangle trees; parkways that were once scenic drives lined by noble trees have become eyesores—corridors of dead trees engulfed in vines.

Just as trees protect our water quality by absorbing storm water and excess nutrients, these invasive plants degrade our water by killing our natural water filtering system. Many of the invasive plants do not have deep roots that help retain soil on stream banks, causing an increase in erosion. Soil erosion adds excess nitrogen and phosphorus to our streams and rivers, causing the unbridled growth of algae and depleting the water of oxygen. This leads to the death of fish and microinvertebrates essential for water quality.

Crowding out our native plants with alien plants in fact threatens all aspects of biodiversity. Native insects are specialists that have co-evolved with native plants for thousands of years. They cannot survive without them. Native birds and amphibians depend on specific insects, so they, too, are threatened, and so on up the food chain.[119] Native oak trees, for example, enrich the natural environment because they are home to lichens, spiders, moths, and many other insects. These attract goldfinches, titmice, nuthatches, woodpeckers, and red-shouldered hawks. Acorns are important to squirrels, deer, and mice.

As gardeners, it may not be possible to eradicate all of the invasive species in our yards, but we can try and keep them at bay. We can cut the vines that would otherwise strangle our trees. Local native plant centers, Audubon chapters, and garden clubs can provide information so you can learn to distinguish the native plants in your area from the non-native ones.

In addition to HABITURF, The Lady Bird Johnson Wildflower and Native Plant Center has a wonderful database for native plants that should thrive with minimal care in every region. We can still plant some non-native plants that we enjoy, as long as they are not aggressive and invasive, and as long as we plant lots of native plants to support our local wildlife. Native plants are well adapted to local conditions, and require much less water during dry months. Our backyards are both essential to wildlife and crucial to protecting our water, so our choices are important.

Rain Gardens

Even if we don't use pesticides or fertilizers, rainwater carries debris from roads, roofs, driveways, sidewalks, and tennis courts that may travel through our yard when it rains. A rain garden—a ditch or depression in the ground that has been planted with native plants—absorbs this polluted runoff, allowing it to be absorbed by the ground and filtered rather than entering a stream or lake. Just as important, a rain garden can prevent flooding by absorbing excess water.

If many homes and businesses in a community have rain gardens, storm water runoff decreases substantially. This is important even in urban areas, where storm water runoff can combine in the sewer system with wastewater. Rain gardens are a simple measure that can help prevent this. Plants that like "wet feet," including ferns and milkweed, will flourish in a rain garden. Milkweed, though much maligned, is a perennial wildflower and—as mentioned earlier—is the only plant that Monarch butterflies can breed on. Swamp milkweeds come in pink and white.

Trees and Shrubs

Native trees and shrubs survive without much watering during dry months and absorb large amounts of water, excess nutrients, and pollutants. They can provide privacy, shade, and habitat for native birds and wildlife. They not only add

GARDEN LEGACY

Ellen Rouse Conrad cultivates much more than hosta, rhubarb, and allium in her Bedford garden, although her flower beds and vegetable garden are admittedly striking. A legacy beyond her family and local community, Conrad's garden has inspired her work with Garden Club of America to drive legislative change to protect our natural world. Conrad's mother introduced her to gardening, and she in turn has brought flowers from her garden to her three children in times of illness, while studying for exams, and later for each of their weddings. She has served her family and friends meals prepared from her garden, and she's organized school vegetable gardens. Visitors to Conrad's garden, wooed by her roses and hospitality, learn how gardening protects our water, the air we breathe, biodiversity, and the hearts and minds of the next generation.

Walking over moss and ferns through the cool woods in the rear of her property, visitors see young trees—protected from deer in eye-catching white plastic tree tubes—on the banks of a meandering river. These young trees were planted with the help of New York City's Watershed Agricultural Council to protect the New York City reservoir, which this river drains into, from erosion and pollutants in rainwater. These trees will absorb carbon for many generations as they grow, protecting our air. As past president of the Bedford Garden Club and founder, along with Mary Beth Kass and Olivia Farr, of the environmental group Bedford 2020, Conrad also uses these trees as a way to educate her community about how our own gardens can help our communities.

Emily Whaley, in her book Mrs. Whaley and Her Charleston Garden, advises gardeners: "Early to bed. Early to rise. Work like hell and fertilize." Well, Conrad would differ on this last point and recommend compost—and this is something you will know before you leave her garden. If she can do it, she says, so can you!

An attorney educated at Radcliffe College and Columbia Law School, Conrad's warm smile and casual air belie her steadfast determination to make use of this education to leave the next generation a verdant, healthy legacy.

to our quality of life, they also provide what are known as "green infrastructure" services. These are big words for simple but important functions.

Street trees are particularly important in towns and cities for preventing flooding and decreasing the amount of storm water entering sewage systems. If town roads are lined with street trees, storm water runoff is markedly diminished, preventing overflowing of storm drains into combined sewer and storm water systems and thereby preventing sewage treatment plants from being overwhelmed. This prevents sewage from entering nearby streams, lakes, and rivers. Trees also help improve water quality when they absorb storm water by capturing excess nutrients and pollutants that would otherwise wash into these water bodies. Elms, oaks, maples, and other long-lived trees that border roads also sequester significant amounts of carbon, helping mitigate greenhouse gasses—and they shelter the roadway, sidewalks, and nearby homes from sun in the summer, making walking more pleasant and decreasing the need for air conditioning.

Meadows

Letting grass grow into a meadow allows wildlife and native grasses to grow and, if mowed once a year after breeding season, provides habitat for native birds. Waves of meadow blowing in the breeze means long roots that can absorb rainwater and nutrients, protecting nearby streams and rivers. To establish a meadow you may need to mow once a month for the first two years, maintaining a height of nine inches or so. This prevents weeds from getting established and allows grasses to gain a foothold. If you have a large meadow, you may want to mow paths through it so you can walk comfortably.

Buffer Areas

Buffer areas of at least 100 feet—more if there are slopes—near streams and wetlands protect the waterways if we allow the grass to grow tall or plant trees and shrubs. Protecting wetland areas is an important way we can protect our water quality and our family's health. New York City's Watershed Agricultural Council supports tree planting in non-forested watershed areas because it is one of the least expensive and most effective ways to protect water quality.

ELIMINATING TOXIC CHEMICALS FROM THE HOME

Household cleaning products we put down the drain make their way to our water supply. Again, as we've learned, not all toxicants get filtered out as water makes its way through the cycle and back to our taps. Though the focus of this book is not on household cleaning products, it would be remiss to not suggest some alternatives to their use, since they infiltrate and contaminate the water supply in much the same way as toxic products used on lawns and in gardens.

Alternative Household Cleaning Solutions

For household cleaning and chores, consider using a few simple ingredients found in your kitchen cupboards. A simple axiom, "like dissolves like," is the key to sensible household cleaning that does not harm the water supply.

VEGETABLE OIL

Fat or greasy material that is not readily water-soluble combines best with other fatty material. Dissolving grease buildup on the bottom of frying pans is often easiest with a little excess vegetable cooking oil when it is warm. This also helps the pan maintain its seasoning. (This method doesn't work well on plates and dishes, where we do not want an oil residue.)

SOAPS AND DETERGENTS

Detergents have bipolar molecules. In other words, detergents have one part that is non-polar and has hydrocarbons that combine with grease, and another part that is charged and combines with water. This helps grease disperse. There are many good "green" choices for soaps on the market that do not have added enzymes, bleaches, oxidizers, and scents.

VINEGAR AND LEMON JUICE

Since both vinegar and lemon juice are weak acids, they are good at cleaning some stubborn stains (though they can also damage finishes). Be sure to test surfaces before use. Neither should be used on "finished" or lacquered metals, including lacquered brass, or on metal coatings, grout, or marble.

Lemon Juice

The juice from half a lemon, combined with a little salt, can clean unlacquered brass, copper pots, and grills. Lemon juice and cream of tartar can remove rust stains from clothes (test first). Cream of tartar is a mildly acidic potassium salt that forms when grapes ferment. Lemon juice can also remove mineral deposits from bathroom fixtures and teapots and is good for cleaning wood cutting boards and killing some bacteria.

Vinegar

Fill a spray bottle with half white vinegar and half water. Use to clean windows, kitchen surfaces, tiles, and soap scum in bathrooms. Vinegar kills some bacteria and destroys unpleasant odors.

BAKING SODA

Baking soda is an excellent abrasive scrub for cleaning kitchen sinks, dishes, pots, and even the refrigerator. It can be stored next to the sink in a powdered sugar dispenser for easy use. Note that mixing it with vinegar or lemon juice neutralizes the mixture and makes it ineffective.

HYDROGEN PEROXIDE

Hydrogen peroxide is excellent at removing blood and food stains, as well as soil, from fabric, but you need to test it first since it can damage or bleach some fabrics. Hydrogen peroxide is an oxidizing agent, which simply means that it accepts an electron from another chemical or reducing agent. In the process of being reduced, the other chemical is transformed into a slightly different state, which makes it easy to remove.

VEGETABLE OIL SOAP

Simple vegetable oil soaps are available that are excellent for cleaning hardwood floors.

PHARMACEUTICAL DISPOSAL

Even though studies find that pharmaceutical drugs are polluting our drinking water and water supply, many pharmacists and hospitals that dispense medicine still promote antiquated directions instructing people to dispose of their unused medications by flushing them down the toilet. Though it may take an extra step, proper disposal of medications is imperative for our health and the health of our water supply. The federal government has a new program called the National Take-Back Initiative. This initiative partners the federal Drug Enforcement Administration (DEA) with local police departments to collect pharmaceuticals, preventing them from being misused and, thus, protecting the water supply. Visit the DEA Office of Diversion Control website for more information on pharmaceutical collection sites.

A FINAL WORD

Change is never easy, but it's made easier through knowledge. In the past, especially in our dealings with toxic substances, we have learned much in hindsight—after the damage had already been done. We have enough knowledge now, however, on the toxic health effects of the substances we use in and around our homes to be proactive and make change. We know that when we use pesticides, weed killers, and fertilizers (and other toxic products), we pollute our water and put ourselves, and those around us, at serious health risk. We also know that our children are most susceptible. Protecting them is easier with this new understanding.

Maintaining water quality is vital to our health and the health of generations to come, and doing our part to improve water quality really is as simple as refraining from using toxic substances in and around our homes.

The Great Healthy Yard Project is not about organic farming or absolutes; it's about making informed choices. You now have an understanding of the water cycle and how these toxic chemicals end up in our drinking water when you use them. You are also armed with research findings and statistics and know how these toxic substances affect the body and whom they affect most. And last, you have been given the tools to maintain your yard without them. The only step left is to apply what you've learned and help educate the wider community by taking "the pledge."

TAKE THE PLEDGE!

Join us in keeping our water healthy! We now know that very small amounts of chemicals, such as synthetic pesticides and fertilizers, can adversely affect human health, causing problems as diverse as autism, ADHD, diabetes, and cancer. If we take care of our yards without these chemicals and do not throw pharmaceuticals and chemicals down our drains and toilets, we are protecting our health and that of our children.

Join us in taking care of your property without synthetic chemical use. If you use a limited local application on rare occasions to wipe out an infestation or improve overall habitat for native wildflowers, birds, and other wildlife, we will still count you as managing with Minimal Impact. Together, we can make a big difference!

"I pledge to take care of my yard without synthetic pesticides, weed killers, or fertilizers, except, on rare occasions, to resolve an infestation or improve habitat for native plants and wildlife. I also pledge not to flush pharmaceutical drugs or household chemicals down drains or toilets."

Our Yards. Our Children. Our Responsibility.

Enlist your neighborhood and friends to take "The Pledge" and share your stories on our website: **www.thegreathealthyyardproject.com** or **www.tghyp.com.**

References

1   EPA National Rivers and Streams Assessment 2008-2009 Collaborative Survey Draft released February 28, 2013, US EPA Office of Wetlands, Oceans and Watersheds, Office of Research and Development, Washington DC 20460, EPA 84/841/D-13/001.

2   United States Geological Survey, Pesticides: Results of the National Assessment of Water Quality Assessment, 2013. http://pubs.usgs.gov/circ/circ1225/pdf/pest.pdf

3   Nneka Leiba, MPH, Analyst; Sean Gray, MS Senior Analyst, Jane Houlihan, MSCE Sr VP for Research, Bottled Water Scorecard 2011, Environmental Working Group.

4   Erik D. Olson, Bottled Water: Pure Drink or Pure Hype?, Apr 1999, Natural Resources Defense Council. http://www.nrdc.org/water/drinking/bw/exesum.asp

5   Tallamy, Douglas, Bringing Nature Home, Timber Press, Portland Oregon, 2007, p.54.

6   Grube A, Donaldson D, Kiely T, Wu L, Pesticide Industry Usage and Sales 2006–2007 Market Estimates, Biological and Economic Analysis Division, United States Environmental Protection Agency, Washington DC Feb. 2011. http://www.epa.gov/opp00001/pestsales/07pestsales/market_estimates2007.pdf

7   Lloyd Smith M, Sheffield Brotherton B, Children's Environmental Health: intergenerational equity in action—a civil society perspective, Ann NY Acad Sci, 2008 Oct: 1140:190 200.

8   Morgan MK, Stout DM, Jones PA, Barr DB, An observational study of the potential for human exposures to pet borne diazinon residues following lawn applications, Environ Res, 2008 Jul; 107(3):336 42.

9   Gore AC, Crews D 2009 Environmental endocrine disruption of brain and behavior. In: Pfaff DW, Arnold AP, Etgen A, Fahrbach S, Rubin R, eds. Hormones, Brain and Behavior, San Diego, Academic Press, pp. 1789-1816

10 Craig GR, Ogilvie DM, Alteration of t maze performance in mice exposed to DDT during pregnancy and lactation, Environ Physiol Biochem, 1974, 4(5):189 199.

11   Johansson U, Fredriksson A, Erickson LL, Low dose effects of paraoxon in adult mice exposed neonatally to DDT: changes in behavioral and cholinergic receptor variables, Environ Toxicol Pharmacol, 1996; 155(4):313-322.

12 McGlynn KA, Abnet CC, Zhang M, Sun XD, Fan JH, O'Brien TR, et al, Serum concentrations of 1,1,1-trichloro-2,2-bis(p-phlorophenyl)ethane (DDT) and 1,1-112 dichloro-2,2-bis(p-chlorophenyl)ethylene (DDE) and risk of primary liver cancer, J Natl Cancer Inst, 2006; 98(14):1005-1010.

13   Garabrant DH, Held J, Langholz B, Peters JM, Mack TM, DDT and related compounds and risk of pancreatic cancer, J Natl Cancer Inst, 1992; 84(10):764-771.

14   Cohn BA, Wolff MS, Cirillo PM, Sholz RI, DDT and breast cancer in young women: new data on the significance of age at exposure, Environ Health Perspect, 2007; 115:1406-1414.

15   Rignell Hydbom A, Rylander L, Hagmar L, Exposure to persistent organochlorine pollutants and type 2 diabetes mellitus, Hum Exp Toxicol, 2007; 26(5):447-452.

16   Morgan DP, Lin LI, Saikaly HH, Morbidity and mortality in workers occupationally exposed to pesticides, Environ Contam Toxicol, 1980; 9(3):349-382.

17   Rull RP, Ritz B, Shaw GM, Neural tube defects and maternal residential proximity to agricultural pesticide applications, Am J Epidemiol, 2006 Apr 15; 163(8)743-53.

18   Clapp RW, Jacobs MM, Loechler EL, Environmental and occupational causes of cancer: new evidence, 2005 2007, Rev Environ Health, 2008 Jan Mar; 23(1):1-37.

19   US Environmental Protection Agency National Primary Drinking Water Regulations, 816-F-09-004, May 2004. http://www.epa.gov/safewater/consumer/pdf/mcl.pdf

20   http://water.epa.gov/drink

21   Biro FM, Galvez MP, Greenspan LC, Succop PA, Vangeepuram N, Pinney SM, Tietlebaum S, Windham GC, Kushi LH, Wolf MS, Pubertal Assessment Method and Baseline Characteristics in a Mixed Longitudinal Study of Girls, Pediatrics, 2010 Sep; 126(3):e583-90. doi: 10.1542/peds.2009-3079.

22   Barnes KK, Kolpin DW, Furlong ET, Zaugg SD, Meyer MT, Barber LB, A national reconnaissance of pharmaceuticals and other organic wastewater contaminants in the US groundwater, Sci Total Environ, 2008 Sep 1; 402(2 3):192-200.

23   Standley LJ, Rudel RA, Swartz CH, Attfield KR, Christian J, Erickson M, Brody JG, Wastewater contaminated groundwater as a source of endogenous hormones and pharmaceuticals to surface water ecosystems, Environ Toxicol Chem, 2008 Dec; 27(12):2457-68.

24   Stackelberg PE, Furlong ET, Meyer MT, Zaugg SD, Henderson AK, Reissman DB, Persistence of pharmaceutical compounds and other organic wastewater contaminants in a conventional drinking water treatment plant, Sci Total Environ 2004 Aug 15; 329(1 3):99-113.

25   Godfrey E, Woessner WW, Benotti MJ, Pharmaceuticals in on site sewage effluent and ground water, Western Montana, Ground Water, 2007 May Jun; 45(3):263-71.

26   Wilcox JD, Bahr JM, Hedman CJ, Hemming JD, Barman MA, Bradbury KR, Removal of organic wastewater contaminants in septic systems using advanced treatment technologies, J Environ Qual 2009 Jan; 13:38(1):149-56.

27   Benotti MJ, Trenholm RA, Vanderford BJ, Hoady JC, Stanford BD, Snyder SA, Pharmaceuticals and endocrine disrupting compounds in US drinking water, Environ Sci Technol, 2009 Feb 1; 43(3):597-603.

28   Freedonia Group, Lawn and Garden Consumables to 2016 – Industry Market Research, Market Share, Market Size, Sales, Demand Forecast, Market Leaders, Company Profiles, Industry Trends, Study # 2891, May 2012.

29   http://water.epa.gov/type/watersheds/whatis.cfm

30   http://water.epa.gov/type/watersheds/whatis.cfm

31   Bay Area Water Supply and Conservation Agency. http://bawsca.org/water-supply/hetch-hetchy-water-system

32   Frances R. Duncombe, Katonah The History of a New York Village and its People, KVIS, 1961; 205-221.

33   New York State 2011 Supplemental Generic Environmental Impact Statement, New York State Department of Health. http://www.dec.ny.gov/press/75403.html

34   Schmidt, Charles W; Blind Rush? Shale Gas Boom Proceeds Amid Human Health Questions; Environ Health Perspect 119:a348-a353 (2011).

35   New York City Department of Environmental Protection, History of New York City's Water Supply System. http://www.nyc.gov/html/dep/html/drinking_water/history.shtml; http://www.nyc.gov/html/nycwater/html/drinking/history.shtml

36   The Environmental Protection Agency, Region 2, New York City Watershed. http://www.epa.gov/region02/water/nycshed

37   New York City Department of Environmental Protection Repair of Delaware Aqueduct Rondout-West Branch Tunnel. http://www.nyc.gov/html/dep/html/dep_projects/cp_delaware_aqueduct_bypass_tunnel.shtml

38   New York City Government Operations, Water Supply Goals, 2011 to 2014. http://www.nyc.gov/html/dep/pdf/strategic_plan/dep_strategy_2011_operations.pdf

39   Environmental Protection Agency, Region 2, Watershed Protection Program. http://www.epa.gov/region2/water/nycshed/protprs.htm

40   Environmental Protection Agency Region 2, New York City Watershed Memorandum of Agreement. http://www.epa.gov/region2/water/nycshed/nycmoa.htm

41   Office of Public Health New York State, Robert Herdman, M.D. Director, Love Canal Public Health Time Bomb, Sept. 1978, pp. 1- 32.

42   http://www.epa.gov/region02/superfund/npl/lovecanal

43   Dieamanti-Kandarakis E et al, 2009 Endocrine-Disrupting chemicals: An Endocrine Society Scientific Statement, Endocrine Reviews 30(4):293-342.

44   Tiido T, Rignell-Hydbom A, Jonsson BA, Giwercman YL, Pedersen HS, Wojtyniak B, Ludwicki JK, Lewovoy V, Zvyezday V, Spano M, Manicardi GC, Bizzaro D, Bonefeld-iorgensen EC, Toft G, Bonde JP, Rylander L, Hagmar L, Giwercman A, Impact of PCB and p,p- DDE contaminants on human sperm Y:X chromosome ratio: studies in three European populations and the Inuit population in Greenland, Environ Health Perspect, 2006 May; 114(5): 718-24.

45   EPA National Rivers and Streams Assessment 2008-2009 Collaborative Survey Draft released February 28, 2013 US EPA Office of Wetlands, Oceans and Watersheds, Office of Research and Development, Washington DC 20460, EPA 84/841/D-13/001.

46   United States Geological Survey, Circular 1225, Pesticides, pp.57-79. http://pubs.usgs.gov/circ/circ1225/pdf/pest.pdf

47   New York City Department of Environmental Protection, Strickland, Carter Commissioner, 2010 Occurrence of Pharmaceuticals and Personal Care Products (PPCPs) in Source Water of the New York City Water Supply, pp. 1-23.

48   http://www.ars.usda.gov/is/np/mba/april97/calepa.htm

49   United States Environmental Protection Agency, 2006-2007 Pesticide Market Estimates, Usage, Sections 3.1-3.10. http://www.epa.gov/opp00001/pestsales/07pestsales/usage2007_3.htm#3_7

50   Grube, Arthur; Donaldson, David; Kiely, Timothy, and Wu, La; United States Environmental Protection Agency, Pesticide Industry Sales and Usage, 2006 and 2007 Market Estimates, Biological and Economic Analysis Division Office of Pesticide Programs, Office of Chemical Safety and Pollution Provention, Washington, DC, Feb. 2011, pp.1-33. http://www.epa.gov/opp00001/pestsales/07pestsales/market_estimates2007.pdf

51   National Pesticide Information Center, Oregon State University, Diazinon Technical Fact Sheet. http://npic.orst.edu/factsheets/diazinontech.html#endo

52   Bouchard MF, Bellinger DC, Wright RO, Weisskopf MG; Attention-deficit/hyperactivity disorder and urinary metabolites of organophosphate pesticides; Pediatrics. 2010 Jun; 125(6):e1270-7. doi: 10.1542/peds.2009-3058. Epub 2010 May 17.

53   United States Environmental Protection Agency, 2006-2007 Pesticide Market Estimates. http://www.epa.gov/opp00001/pestsales/07pestsales/usage2007_3.htm#3_7

54   National Pesticide Information Center Oregon State University, Carbaryl Fact Sheet. http://npic.orst.edu/factsheets/carbgen.pdf

55   Megan K Horton PhD, Andrew Rundle PhD, David E Camann MS, Dana Boyd Barr PhD, Virginia A Rauh ScD, and Robin M Whyatt PhD; Impact of Prenatal Exposure to Piperonyl Butoxide and Perethrin on 36-month Neurodevelopment; Pediatrics. 2011 March; 127(3): 699¬706.

56   Grube, Arthur; Donaldson, David; Kiely, Timothy, and Wu, La; United States Environmental Protection Agency, Pesticide Industry Sales and Usage, 2006 and 2007 Market Estimates, Biological and Economic Analysis Division Office of Pesticide Programs, Office of Chemical Safety and Pollution Provention, Washington, DC, Feb. 2011, pp.1-33.

57   Rignell-Hydbom A, Rylander L, Giwercman A, Jonsson BA, Nilsson-Ehle P, Hagmar L, Exposure to CB-153 and p,p'-DDE and male reproductive function, Hum Reprod, 2004 Sep; 19(9): 2066-75.

58   Montgomery MP, Kamel F, Saldana TM, Alavania MC, Sandler DP, Incident diabetes and pesticide exposure among licensed pesticide applicators: Agricultural Health study, 1993-2003, Am J Epidemiol, 2008 May15;167(10):1235-46.

59   Mrema EJ, Rubino FM, Brambilla G, Moretto A, Tsatsakis AM, Colosio C, Persistent organo-chlorinated pesticides and mechanisms of their toxicity, Toxicology, 2013 May 10; 307:74-88. doi: 10.1016/j.tox.2012.11.015.

60   Schug TT, Janesick A, Blumberg B, Heindel JJ, Endocrine disrupting chemicals and disease suscepti-bility, J Steroid Biochem Mol Biol. 2011 Nov; 127(3-5):204-15. doi: 10.1016/j.jsbmb.2011.08.007.

61   Bratton MR, Frigo DE, Segar HC, Nephew KP, McLachlan JA, Wiese TE, Burow ME, Depart-ment of Pharmacology, Tulane University, New Orleans, Louisiana, USA. The organochlorine o,p'-DDT plays a role in coactivator-mediated MAPK crosstalk in MCF-7 breast cancer cells, Environ Health Perspect, 2012 Sep; 120(9):1291-6. doi: 10.1289/ehp.1104296.

62   Zhao B, Shen H, Liu F, Liu S, Niu J, Guo F, Sun X, Medical College of Xiamen University, Xiamen 361005, PRC, Exposure to organochlorine pesticides is an independent risk factor of hepatocellular carcinoma: a case-control study, J Expo Sci Environ Epidemiol. 2012 Nov; 22(6):541-8. doi: 10.1038/jes.2011.29.

63   Hoppin JA, Tolbert PE, Holly EA, Brock JW, Korrick SA, Altshul LM, Zhang RH, Bracci PM, Burse VW, Needham LL, Pancreatic cancer and serum organochlorine levels, Cancer Epidemiol Biomarkers Department of Environmental and Occupational Health, Rollins School of Public Health, Emory University, Atlanta, Georgia 30322, USA, Prev. 2000 Feb; 9(2):199-205.

64   United States Environmental Protection Agency http://www.epa.gov/kidshometour/products/wkill.htm

65   United States Environmental Protection Agency, Causual/Analysis, Diagnosis, Decision Information System, Herbicides, Volume 2: Sources, Stressors and Responses. http://www.epa.gov/caddis/ssr_herb_int.html

66   Gasnier C, Dumont C, Benachour N, Clair E, Chagnon MC, Séralini GE, Glyphosate-based herbicides are toxic and endocrine disruptors in human cell lines, University of Caen, Institute of Biology, Lab. Biochemistry EA2608, Esplanade de la Paix, 14032 Caen cedex, France. Toxicology. 2009 Aug 21; 262(3):184-91.

67   United States Environmental Protection Agency, Causual/Analysis, Diagnosis, Decision Information System, Herbicides, Volume 2: Sources, Stressors and Responses. http://www.epa.gov/caddis/ssr_herb_int.html

68   United States Environmental Protection Agency, Pesticide Re-registration, Tolerance and Reassessment Progress and Risk Management Decision, Tolerance Re-registration Eligibility Decision, Diquat Dibromide. http://www.epa.gov/oppsrrd1/REDs/factsheets/diquat_tred_fs.htm

69   Knobeloch L, Salna B, Hogan A, Postle J, Anderson H, Blue babies and nitrate-contaminated well water; Environ Health Perspect. 2000 Jul; 108(7):675-8.

70   Catsburg CE, Gago-Dominguez M, Yuan JM, Castelao JE, Cortessis VK, Pike MC, Stern MC,

Department of Preventive Medicine, Keck School of Medicine, Norris Comprehensive Cancer Center, University of Southern California, Los Angeles, CA, Dietary sources of N-nitroso compounds and bladder cancer risk: Findings from the Los Angeles bladder cancer study, Int J Cancer. 2013 Jun 18; doi: 10.1002/ijc.28331.

71   Hannas BR, Das PC, Li H, LeBlanc GA, Department of Environmental & Molecular Toxicology, North Carolina State University, Raleigh, North Carolina, United States of America., Intracellular conversion of environmental nitrate and nitrite to nitric oxide with resulting developmental toxicity to the crustacean Daphnia magna., PLoS One. 2010 Aug 27; 5(8):e12453. doi: 10.1371/journal.pone.0012453.

72   http://www.epa.gov/iaq/voc.html

73   http://www.epa.gov/iaq/voc.html#Health%20Effects

74   Starek A, Szabla I, Ethylene glycol alkyl ethers the substances noxious to health, Med Pr, 2008; 59(2):179-85.

75   Schecter A, Shah N, Colacino JA, Brummitt SI, Ramakrishnan V, Robert Harris T, Papke O, PBDEs in US and German clothes dryer lint: a potential source of indoor contamination and exposure, Chemosphere, 2009 May; 75(5):623-8.

76   Schmeiser HH, Gminski R, Mersch Sundermann V, Evaluation of health risks caused by musk ketone, Internat J of Hygiene and Environmental Health, 2001. 203(4):293-299.

77   Zogorski JS, Carter JM, Ivahnenko T, Lapham WW, Moran MJ, Rowe BL, Squillace PJ, Toccalina PL, The quality of our nations waters: volatile organic compounds in the nations ground water and drinking water supply wells, USGS Circular 1292. http://pubs.usgs.gov/circ/circ1292/pdf/circular1292.pdf

78   Personal communication with Keri Powell.

79   Carter H. Strickland, Jr. Commissioner, NYC Environmental Protection, 2010 Occurrence of Pharmaceuticals and Personal Care Products (PPCPs) in Source Water of the New York City Water Supply. http://www.nyc.gov/html/dep/pdf/quality/nyc_dep_2010_ppcpreport.pdf

80   Standley LJ, Rudel RA, Swartz CH, Attfield KR, Christian J, Erickson M, Brody JG, Wastewater contaminated groundwater as a source of endogenous hormones and pharmaceuticals to surface water ecosystems, Environ Toxicol Chem, 2008 Dec; 27(12):2457-68.

81   Barnes KK, Kolpin DW, Furlong ET, Zaugg SD, Meyer MT, Barber LB, A national reconnaissance of pharmaceuticals and other organic wastewater contaminants in the US groundwater, Sci Total Environ, 2008 Sep 1; 402(2 3):192-200.

82   Stackelberg PE, Furlong ET, Meyer MT, Zaugg SD, Henderson AK, Reissman DB, Persistence of pharmaceutical compounds and other organic wastewater contaminants in a conventional drinking water treatment plant, Sci Total Environ, 2004 Aug 15; 329(1 3):99-113.

83   Godfrey E, Woessner WW, Benotti MJ, Pharmaceuticals in on site sewage effluent and ground water, Western Montana, Ground Water, 2007 May Jun; 45(3):263-71.

84   Wilcox JD, Bahr JM, Hedman CJ, Hemming JD, Barman MA, Bradbury KR, Removal of organic wastewater contaminants in septic systems using advanced treatment technologies, J Environ Qual, 2009 Jan 13; 38(1):149-56.

85   Benotti MJ, Trenholm RA, Vanderford BJ, Hoady JC, Stanford BD, Snyder SA, Pharmaceuticals and endocrine disrupting compounds in US drinking water, Environ Sci Technol, 2009 Feb 1; 43(3):597 603.

86   Wooster R, Neuhausen SL, Mangion J, Quirk Y, Ford D, Collins N, Nguyen K, Seal S, Tran T, Averill D, et al, Localization of a breast cancer susceptibility gene BRCA2, to chromosome 13q12-13, Science, 1994 Sept 30; 265.No5181: pp. 2088-2090.

87   Mañas F, Peralta L, Raviolo J, García Ovando H, Weyers A, Ugnia L, Gonzalez Cid M, Larripa I, Gorla N., Genotoxicity of AMPA, the environmental metabolite of glyphosate, assessed by the Comet assay and cytogenetic tests. Ecotoxicol Environ Saf. 2009 Mar; 72(3):834-7. doi: 10.1016/j.ecoenv.2008.09.019. Epub 2008 Nov 14.

88   http://www.epa.gov/hudson

89   http://www.epa.gov/history/topics/pcbs/01.htm

90   http://www.epa.gov/Region5/sites/waukegan/index.htm

91   Forger NG, Control of cell number in the sexually dimorphic brain and spinal cord, J Neuroen-docrinol, 2009 Mar; 21(4):393-9.

92   Parisaul HB, Todd KL, Mickens JA, Adewale HB, Impact of neonatal exposure to the ERalpha agonist PPT, bisphenol A or phytoestrogens on hypothalamic kesspeptin fiber density in male and female rats, Neurotoxicology, 2009 May; 30(3):350-7.

93   Swan SH, Brazil C, Drobnis EZ, Liu F, Kruse RL, Hatch M, Redmon JB, Wang C, Overstreet JW, Geographic differences in semen quality of fertile US males, Environ Health Perspect, 2003 Apr; 111(4): 414-20.

94   Joensen UN, bossi R, Leffers H, Jensen AA, Skakkebaek NE, Iorgensen N, Do perflouroalkyl compounds impair human semen quality? Environ Health Perspect, 2009 Jun; 117(6):923-7.

95   Fisher JS, Environmental ant-androgens and male reproductive health: focus on phthalates and testicular dysgenesis syndrome, Reproduction, 2004 Mar; 127(3):305-15.

96   Jugan ML, Levi Y, Blondeau JP, Endocrine disruptors and thyroid hormone physiology, Biochem Pharmacol, 2009 Nov 11.

97   Jacobson JL, Jacobson SW, Intellectual impairment in children exposed to polychlorinated biphenyls in utero, N Engl J Med 1996 Sep 12; 335(11):783-9.

98   Patandin S, Lanting Cl, Mulder PG, Boersman ER, Sauer PL, Weisglas-Kuperus N, Effects of environmental exposure to polychlorinated biphenyls and dioxins on cognitive abilities in Dutch children at 42 months of age, J Pediatr 1999 Jan; 134(1):33-41.

99   Langer P, Taitakova M, Fodor G, Kocan a, Bohov P, Michalek J, Kreze A, Increased thyroid volume and prevalence of thyroid disorders in an area heavily polluted by polychlorinated biphenyls, Eur J Endocrinol, 1998 Oct; 139(4):402-9.

100   de Cock M, Maas YG, van de Bor M., Does perinatal exposure to endocrine disruptors induce autism spectrum and attention deficit hyperactivity disorders? Review, Acta Paediatr. 2012 Aug; 101(8):811-8. doi: 10.1111/j.1651-2227.2012.02693.x.

101   Román GC, Ghassabian A, Bongers-Schokking JJ, Jaddoe VW, Hofman A, de Rijke YB, Verhulst FC, Tiemeier H., Association of gestational maternal hypothyroxinemia and increased autism risk., Ann Neurol. 2013 Aug 13; doi: 10.1002/ana.23976.

102   Theo Colborn, Neurodevelopment and Endocrine Disruption, Envir. Health Perspect, 2004 Jun; 112(9):944-949

103   Howdeshell KL, A model of the development of the brain as a construct of the thyroid system. Environ Health Perspect, 2002 Jun; 110 Suppl 3:337-48.

104   Goldey ES, Kehn LS, Lau C, Rehnberg GL, Crofton KM, Developmental exposure to polychlorinated biphenyls (Aroclor 1254) reduces circulating thyroid hormone concentrations and causes hearing deficits in rats, Toxicol Appl Pharmacol, 1995 Nov; 135(1):77-88.

105   Weiss RE, Stein MA, Trommer B, Refetoff S, Attention-deficit hyperactivity disorder and thyroid function, J Pediatr. 1993 Oct; 123(4):539-45.

106   Rodier PM, Ingram JL, Tisdale B, Nelson S, Romano J, Embryological origin for autism: developmental anomalies of the cranial nerve motor nuclei J Comp Neurol, 1996 Jun 24; 370(2):247-61.

107   Turyk M, Anderson HS, Knobeloch L, Imm P, Persky VW, Prevalence of diabetes and body burdens of polychlorinated biphenyls, polybrominated dephenyl ethers, and p,p' diphenyldichloroethene in Great Lakes sport fish consumers, Chemosphere, 2009 May; 75(5):674-9.

108   Montgomery MP, Kamel F, Saldana TM, Alvania MC, Sandler DP, Incident Diabetes and pesti-

cide exposure among licensed pesticide applicators: Agricultural Health Study, 1993 2003, Am J Epidemiol, 2008 May; 15:167(10):1235.

109   Rubin BS, Murray MK, Damassa DA, King JC, Soto AM, Perinatal exposure to low doses of bisphenol A affects body weight, patterns of estrous cyclicity, and plasma LH levels, Environ Health Perspect 2001 Jul; 109(7):675-80.

110   Montgomery MP, Kamel F, Saldana TM, Alavania MC, Sandler DP, Incident diabetes and pesticide exposure among licensed pesticide applicators: Agricultural Health study, 1993 2003, Am J Epidemiol, 2008 May15; 167(10):1235-46.

111   http://www.cdc.gov/DES/consumers/about/update.html

112   Herbst AL, Ulfelder H, Poskanzer DC, Adenocarcinoma of the vagina, Association of maternal stilbesterol therapy with tumor appearance in young women, N Engl J Med, 1971; 284:878-881.

113   Palmer JR, Hatch EE, Rosenberg CL, Harge P, Kaufman RH, Titus Ernstoff L, Noller KL, Herbst AL, Rao RS, Troisi R, et al, Risk of breast cancer in women exposed to diethylstilbesterol in utero: preliminary results (US), Cancer Causes Control, 2002; 13:753-758.

114   Rubin MM, Antenatal exposure to DES: lessons learned…future concerns, Obstet Gynecol Sury, 2007 Aug; 62(8):548-55.

115   Grube, Arthur; Donaldson, David; Kiely, Timothy, and Wu, La; United States Environmental Protection Agency, Pesticide Industry Sales and Usage, 2006 and 2007 Market Estimates, Biological and Economic Analysis Division Office of Pesticide Programs, Office of Chemical Safety and Pollution Provention, Washington, DC, Feb 2011, pp.1-33.

116   Personal communication, Mary Thurn, Cornell University Department of Horticulture.

117   All of the Ed Giobbi recipes are from personal communication with Ed Giobbi and printed with his permission.

118   Shirer, Rebecca and Zimmerman, Chris; Forest Regeneration in New York State; The Nature Conservancy Eastern New York; Sep 2010; pp. 1- 25.

119   Tallamy, Douglas; Bringing Nature Home; Timber Press, Portland, Oregon; 2007.

Photo Credits

Page 1: soil under grass, © andreykuzmin/123rf.com

Page 2: green floral pattern, © pavalena/123rf.com

Page 3: boy planting seeds in a vegetable garden, © racorn/123rf.com

Page 4: Black Eyed Susan flowers, © Denny Phillips /123rf.com

Page 5: Echinacea flowers, © Elena Elisseeva/123rf.com

Page 7: vegetables in a garden, © udra/123rf.com

Page 8: bee on a flower, © szefei/123rf.com

Page 9: grass, © Denys Prokofyev/123rf.com

Page 10: Hudson River, © Diane Lewis. The Hudson River is much cleaner now than in the 1970s.

Page 14 (left): Watershed map for the town of Bedford NY prepared for Bedford 2020 by the Westchester Land Trust. Photo © Kara Alderiso of Westchester Land Trust.

Page 14 (right): Children planting trees, © Diane Lewis. Bedford 2020 and the Watershed Agricultural Council partner to plant trees with students on their campus.

Page 16: Children playing in yard, © Brett Molé

Page 18 (left): Water from hose, © Brett Molé

Page 18 (right): Sunflower, © Brett Molé

Page 19 (left): butterfly on flower, © Roman Rak/123rf.com

Page 19 (right): Yard runoff goes into pond, © Diane Lewis. Rainwater washes pesticides and fertilizers applied to this yard into the pond. This pond then drains into a reservoir of a major city.

Page 21: water, © Aaron Amat/123rf.com

Page 22 (left): Glass with clear water, © Brett Molé. Because we can't see most of the pollutants in our drinking water, it is easy to disregard them.

Page 22 (right): DDT CT 1950 CDC (public health image library (PHIL) #2464 no copyright restrictions, in the public domain), photo © CDC. In the 1950's DDT was considered safe enough for residential use. It is now banned in the United States.

Page 24: Lawn pesticide sign, © Brett Mol. Pesticide residues do not disappear after 72 hours. Some remain on the lawn and some are washed into streams and ponds or absorbed with rainwater into groundwater aquifers.

Page 27: Tree tubes, © Diane Lewis. Tree tubes protect young trees and also draw public attention to a student project. These trees will protect the water in this pond and the reservoir that it drains into.

Page 30: Spray bottles, © Brett Molé

Page 33: Native Annabelle with clematis, © Diane Lewis. A healthy yard can have non-native plants mixed with native plants, as long as the foreigners are not invasive. Here native Annabelle hydrangeas intertwine with non-native clematis Comtesse de Bouchaud.

Page 35 (top): Boy, © Brett Molé. How we garden is important to our children's health.

Page 35 (bottom): Dog rolling on lawn, © Diane Lewis. Healthy yards are healthy for our pets, too.

Page 36: Hetch Hetchy Reservoir, © Anton Foltin/123rf.com

Page 39: One Bryant Park, Bank of America Building, © Jack Aiello/123rf.com

Page 43: Cattails, © Diane Lewis. Cattails absorb excess nutrients and pollutants protecting nearby water. They also provide habitat and cover for many wetland animals and birds.

Page 45 (left): Water filtration, © Diane Lewis. Drinking water filtration at small municipal treatment facility.

Page 45 (right): UV disinfection, © Diane Lewis. Ultraviolet disinfection at a drinking water treatment facility.

Page 47: Hetch Hetchy Dam In Yosemite National Park, © videowokart/123rf.com

Page 52: Small municipal wastewater treatment plant, © Diane Lewis.

Page 54: stop sign to No Fracking, © Udo Schotten/123rf.com

Page 56: NYC watershed map. Map: New York City Department of Environmental Protection
New York City's Water Supply System carries water from less densely populated areas to city residents.

Page 60: red onion plant being sprayed, © khunaspix/123rf.com

Page 64: Green and yellow spray bottle, © Brett Molé

Page 66 (left): Ant on flower, © Glenne Gina, U.S. Fish and Wildlife Service/Wikimedia Commons. Ants are one of the most common reasons people use insecticides in their yards.

Page 66 (right): Honeybee on flower, © Diane Lewis. Pesticides kill good insects such as bees that are needed to pollinate food.

Page 69: Ball and stick model of DDT, © petarg/123rf.com

Page 70 (left): Barberry plant, © Chris Hill/123rf.com. Japanese Barberry crowds out native trees and shrubs preventing forest regeneration. The plant is spread by birds dispersing seeds and root runners that stretch out laterally.

Page 70 (right): Milkweed, © Diane Lewis. Milkweed is the only plant that Monarch butterfly eggs can develop on.

Page 77: spray cleaning a window, © Kasia Bialasiewicz/123rf.com

Page 85: Endocrine disruptors graphic, © Diane Lewis. Normally hormones travel in the blood to target cells where they bind to specific receptors. This binding elicits a response. Hormone mimics bind to these receptors and cause continued response, whereas hormone blockers take up the receptor but don't cause a response.

Page 91 (top): spraying herbicide, © Sunisa Chukly/123rf.com

Page 91 (bottom): hand holding a small maple tree, © Charles Wollertz /123rf.com

Page 92: lawn sprinkler, © frogtravel/123rf.com

Page 95: Natural lawn and garden care is easy, © Diane Lewis. A yard cared for without chemicals.

Page 96 (left): Aerator, © Diane Lewis. Using a core aerator is easy, and an aerator can be rented.

Page 96 (right): Cores, © Diane Lewis. Aerating relieves compaction by removing cores. This allows the soil to loosen up so air can penetrate.

Page 100 (left): Vegetable garden, © Diane Lewis. Most people don't spray pesticides on backyard vegetable gardens where their children are going to eat the food because the connection is so direct.

Page 100 (right): Tomatoes, © Diane Lewis. Organically grown tomatoes from a backyard vegetable garden.

Page 101 (left): fresh lemon balm in an organic herbal garden, © Nutthawit Wiangya/123rf.com

Page 101 (right): Chickens on a lawn, © Diane Lewis. Chickens keep the insects at bay in this yard.

Page 102: Ed Giobbi, © Diane Lewis. Ed Giobbi in his vegetable garden. His art studio is in the background.

Page 105: field of dandelions, © Elena Volkova/123rf.com

Page 106: Compost, © Diane Lewis. A backyard compost pile with greens from both the garden and the table and also with chicken manure, will be ready to enrich the garden beds in the spring.

Page 108: Echinacea with a bee, © Diane Lewis. A bee enjoying native Echinacea.

Page 110 (left): Oak tree, © Diane Lewis. A native oak provides habitat for insects and birds, and acorns for deer and mice.

Page 110 (right): Pileated woodpecker, © Brad Thompson/123rf.com. Pileated woodpeckers rely on insects they harvest from trees. Trees also provide a place to nest.

Page 111: Rain garden, © Diane Lewis. This Town House rain garden educates the community as well as increasing water absorption.

Page 113: Ellen Conrad with daughters Francis and Louisa, © Diane Lewis. Ellen Conrad in her garden with daughters Francis and Louisa.

Page 119: Rudbeckia, © oapril/123rf.com

Page 120: montage of vegetable gardens, © annete/123rf.com

Page 140: Young girl looking through viewfinder of her camera making a photo of spring flowers, © Chris Ohlmann/123rf.com

Page 146: gardener, © Alexander Raths/123rf.com

Page 148: Diane Lewis author photo © Danielle Sinclair

Acknowledgments

The friends I have made while working to improve the environment are some of the treasures of my life. I have had the good fortune to learn from and work with truly amazing people, and this book rests on their shoulders. Many of these people have been women, and that is not because these accomplished women have time on their hands—it is because many women seem to intuitively understand the connection between our health and the environment, and because many women are gardeners. The big three at Bedford 2020—Ellen Conrad, Olivia Farr, and Mary Beth Kass—and also Lee Roberts, are so organized, thoughtful, and kind. I will always strive to emulate them in these aspects. They have supported my work, and in doing so have made this book possible.

With her passion, enthusiasm, and keen insight, Allison Rockefeller, founder of Audubon Women in Conservation, has been inspirational, helping me believe that together, all of the work so many of us are doing for the environment will make a difference. Allison also makes it really fun to do good things!

Dianne Stern, whose work as a board member at Earthjustice has helped keep all of our water cleaner, has taught me that legislative and political action is critical to protecting our resources and, in fact, to shaping our society.

In the light of these contributions, it is so fitting that this book is published by She Writes Press. The women I have worked with there, including my editor Liz Kracht, have been instrumental in seeing this project to its fruition.

About the Author

Diane Lewis, MD is an internist and nephrologist. An environmental activist, Lewis has embraced education as a means for implementing change. Lewis graduated from Bryn Mawr College, where she majored in physics and attended Albert Einstein College of Medicine. She completed her residency in internal medicine, as well as her fellowship in nephrology, at Montefiore Medical Center. She is licensed to practice medicine in New York State.

Lewis has lived in the northern suburbs of New York City, where she raised her three children, for the past thirty years. A one-time organic farmer, Lewis has been active in her community, serving on the board of the Katonah Village Improvement Society, America's oldest community group; she is a past board member of the Bedford Audubon Society, and is a member of the Bedford Garden Club. She is also a freelance reporter, contributing environmental articles to the Bedford Record Review, a weekly newspaper.

Lewis is also a board member and chair of the Water and Land Use Task Force of Bedford 2020, a nonprofit tasked with forming a liaison between the community and local government to implement Bedford, New York's Climate Action Plan. She is also a member of the Rachel Carson Awards Council for Audubon Women in Conservation, a member of the Mid-Hudson Regional Sustainability Plan Water Management Working Group, the Town of Bedford Open Space Acquisition Committee, and the Town of Bedford Planning Board. Lewis speaks regularly on the impact of water quality on health.

SELECTED TITLES FROM SHE WRITES PRESS

She Writes Press is an independent publishing company founded to serve women writers everywhere.

Visit us at www.shewritespress.com.

Hedgebrook Cookbook: Celebrating Radical Hospitality by Denise Barr & Julie Rosten. $24.95, 978-1-938314-22-3. Delectable recipes and inspiring writing, straight from Hedgebrook's farmhouse table to yours.

Away from the Kitchen: Untold Stories, Private Menus, Guarded Recipes, and Insider Tips by Dawn Blume Hawkes. $24.95, 978-1-938314-36-0. A food book for those who want it all: the menus, the recipes, *and* the behind-the-scenes scoop on some of America's favorite chefs.

Tasting Home: Coming of Age in the Kitchen by Judith Newton. $16.95, 978-1-938314-03-2. An extraordinary journey through the cuisines, cultures, and politics of the 1940s through 2011, complete with recipes.

Seasons Among the Vines: Life Lessons from the California Wine Country and Paris by Paula Moulton. $16.95, 978-1-938314-16-2. New advice on wine making, tasting, and food pairing—along with a spirited account of the author's experiences in Le Cordon Bleu's pilot wine program—make this second edition even better than the first.

Four Funerals and a Wedding: Resilience in a Time of Grief by Jill Smolowe. $16.95, 978-1-938314-72-8. When journalist Jill Smolowe lost four family members in less than two years, she turned to modern bereavement research for answers—and made some surprising discoveries.

Think Better. Live Better. 5 Steps to Creating the Life You Deserve by Francine Huss. $16.95, 978-1-938314-66-7. With the help of this guide, readers will learn to cultivate more creative thoughts, realign their mindset, and gain a new perspective on life.